· T R O P H I E S ·

Intervention
PRACTICE BOOK
Grade 5

Harcourt

Orlando   Boston   Dallas   Chicago   San Diego

Visit *The Learning Site!*
www.harcourtschool.com

Printed in the United States of America

ISBN 0-15-326153-6

5 6 7 8 9 10 054 10 09 08 07 06 05 04

Table of Contents

Fluency Builder

authority	one	box
souvenir	asked	lines
incredible	were	swam
vow	with	fishing
commotion	knows	Ingrid
exhausted	really	poles
	again	game

1. Ingrid knows / an incredible amount / about fishing, / so she's an authority.

2. "Ingrid, / have you been fishing / again?" / asked Sam.

3. "I would have that huge one stuffed / as a souvenir / if I were you," / he said.

4. "Really?" / Ingrid asked / as she put her fishing lines / and poles / in her tackle box.

5. Suddenly, / there was a big commotion. / The fish started flopping, / knocking Ingrid's tackle box / to the ground.

6. With an incredible effort, / the exhausted fish flipped / and flopped / into the river / and swam away.

7. Ingrid and Sam made a vow / to play a game tomorrow, / instead of fishing.

Harcourt

Name _____

A Fish Tale

Do what the sentences tell you.

June _____

Dan _____   Mike _____

1. Find Dan. He has a *D* on his cap. Write *Dan* on the line by him.
2. Find Mike. He has an *M* on his cap. Write *Mike* on the line by him.
3. Dan has no rod to catch fish with. Make a fishing rod in his hand.
4. Mike likes to fish with a stick and a string. Make a pole for him to fish with.
5. Find June. Make a line from one of her hands to the other.
6. Then draw a fish on the line.
7. Make five stripes on the fish.
8. Make some waves on the lake.
9. Draw a big pine on a sand dune by Dan.
10. Find the ring of stones. Make a blaze in it.
11. Make a plume of smoke going up from the blaze.
12. Find the pup. Make a mat for the pup to nap on.

Write a word from above that has the same vowel sound and spelling pattern as each word below.

13. tune _dune, plume, June_

14. bike _Mike, likes, five, line, stripes, pine_

15. haze _make, waves, lake, blaze_

16. joke _pole, stones, smoke_

Harcourt

Name _____

A Fish Tale

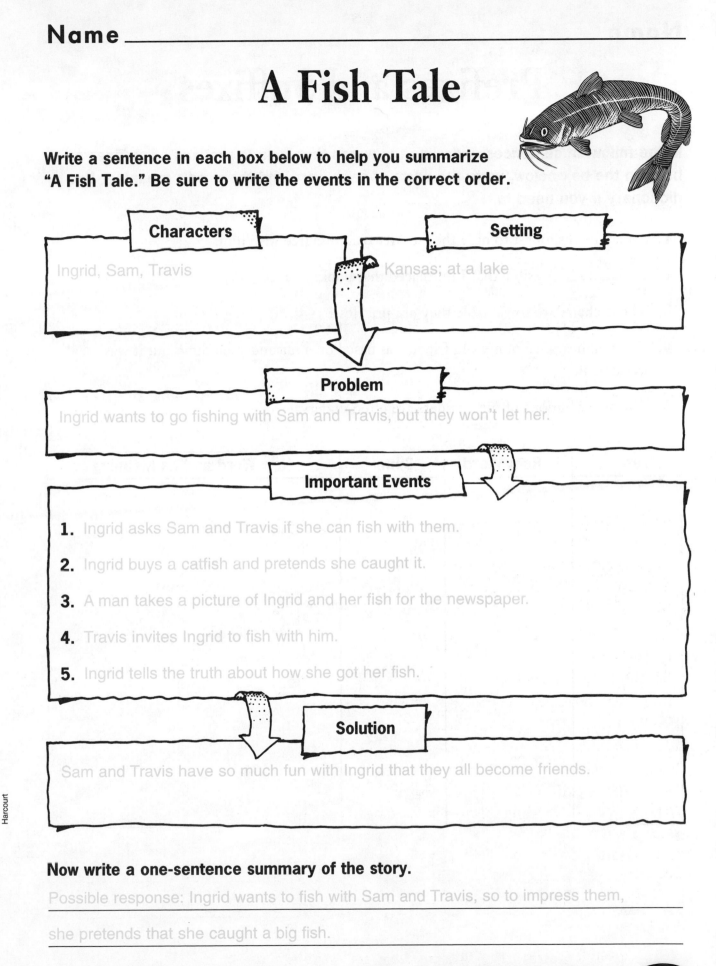

Write a sentence in each box below to help you summarize
"A Fish Tale." Be sure to write the events in the correct order.

Characters

Ingrid, Sam, Travis

Setting

Kansas; at a lake

Problem

Ingrid wants to go fishing with Sam and Travis, but they won't let her.

Important Events

1. Ingrid asks Sam and Travis if she can fish with them.

2. Ingrid buys a catfish and pretends she caught it.

3. A man takes a picture of Ingrid and her fish for the newspaper.

4. Travis invites Ingrid to fish with him.

5. Ingrid tells the truth about how she got her fish.

Solution

Sam and Travis have so much fun with Ingrid that they all become friends.

Now write a one-sentence summary of the story.

Possible response: Ingrid wants to fish with Sam and Travis, so to impress them,

she pretends that she caught a big fish.

Harcourt

Prefixes and Suffixes

In the following sentences underline the words that include prefixes or suffixes or both. In the box below, write the parts of each word and the word's meaning. Use a dictionary if you need to.

1. It may be <u>dishonest</u> to hide the fact that you <u>disagree</u> with him.

2. I think it's <u>impossible</u> that I <u>misplaced</u> that book.

3. Those chairs are so <u>valuable</u> they are <u>priceless</u>.

4. The <u>reappearance</u> of my old friend was based on a <u>misunderstanding</u>, but it was <u>wonderful</u>.

5. The <u>contributions</u> of fifth graders are often <u>undervalued</u>.

Prefix	Root Word	Suffix	New Word and Its Meaning
dis	honest		dishonest–not honest
dis	agree		disagree–not in agreement
im	poss	ible	impossible–not possible
mis	placed		misplaced–wrongly placed
	valu	able	valuable–having value
	price	less	priceless–worth more than any price
re	appear	ance	reappearance–appear again
mis	understanding		misunderstanding–understanding incorrectly
	wonder	ful	wonderful–full of wonder
	contribu	tions	contributions–acts of contributing
under	valued		undervalued–below value

Harcourt

Fluency Builder

tread	when	shed
moss	coming	tree
sternly	knew	scent
compose	hear	creek
exaggerate	then	west
quiver	put	breeze
	was	feel

1. When he had lost his quiver, / he was heading west / toward the creek.

2. He knew / that his father would sternly punish him / if he came home without it.

3. He searched / around the moss covered / tree stumps.

4. He had promised himself / that he would not shed a tear, / but he could feel them / streaming down his face.

5. He had to compose himself, / or he would never find / his quiver.

6. Then the breeze / brought the scent / of something / unfamiliar.

7. Someone was coming. / He could hear / the soft tread / of a boy.

8. With exaggerated movements, / the boy / carefully / put the quiver / on the ground.

The Quiver

Write the word that makes the sentence tell about the picture.

1. Janet has a _____pet_____ finch named Flute.

      vest   pet   jet

2. She puts _____seeds_____ in Flute's dish.

    seeds   feet   weeds

3. Flute likes to hit her bell and _____keys_____.

      keys   honey   jockey

4. She _____tweets_____ a nice tune when it's time for lunch.

  tweets   jeeps   beets

5. Sometimes Janet must _____clean_____ Flute's home.

     leap   clean   deal

6. At bedtime, Flute _____sleeps_____ on her swing.

    weeds   speeds   sleeps

7. Flute _____seems_____ to like her home.

   speeds   seems   bees

The Quiver

Complete the sequence chart about "The Quiver." Write a sentence in each box. The first one is done for you.

Event 1:

Will finds a quiver and gets lost while looking for more things.

Event 2:

Possible response: Will sees another boy looking for something.

Event 3:

Possible response: Will realizes he is looking for the quiver and gives it to him.

Event 4:

Possible response: The boy helps Will find his parents.

Narrative Elements

Read the story, and fill in the blanks.

Jill and Jeri planted a vegetable garden in Jill's backyard. They found a corner of the yard where Mom used to plant flowers. Mom said the girls could use that section for their garden. After they planted six rows of beans, two rows of tomatoes, and one row of lettuce, they kept the plants watered and pulled out the weeds. After a couple of weeks, the beans and tomatoes were growing well, but the lettuce was only one inch high. They inspected the leaves, and there were no bugs on the lettuce. They explained the problem to Dad. He wasn't sure what the problem was but told them he saw a rabbit in the yard the other day. Jill and Jeri decided to build a small fence around the lettuce to keep the rabbit out of the garden.

Characters: Jill, Jeri, Mom, Dad

Setting: a vegetable garden in Jill's backyard

Problem or Conflict: The lettuce was not growing well.

Solution: Jill and Jeri decided to build a fence around the lettuce, as Dad said he had seen a rabbit in the yard.

Harcourt

Fluency Builder

audition	fill	hall
sonata	look	halt
accompaniment	was	wall
accompanist	one	waltz
grimaced	they	called
simultaneously	began	Aldo
	fill	
	came	

1. Jean looked / at the clock / on the wall.

2. The audition / was scheduled to begin / at ten o'clock.

3. Jean planned / to play a waltz / for the audition.

4. Miss Small called on students / to audition / one at a time.

5. Aldo nodded to the accompanist, / a pianist, / and they began to play / simultaneously.

6. The notes of a sonata / filled the hall.

7. When Aldo suddenly jumped up, / the accompaniment came to a halt.

8. Aldo grimaced / because one of his cello strings / had broken.

Name _____

The Audition

Read the story. Circle the words with the vowel sound you hear in *salt*, *hall*, or *stalk*.

(Walt) is now six feet (tall.)	He needs to (walk) to the (mall) to get longer pants.	He (calls) Beth to make a plan: "I'll get you a (malt) if you come with me to the (mall.)"
Then Beth (talks.) She tells (Walt) that the (baseball) game has ended. "I'll meet you at the stone (wall) next to the lake at three."	(Walt) hangs up. When he (walks) outside, the crisp (fall) breeze makes him smile.	(Walt) meets Beth at the stone (wall) at three. He gets her a (malt) at a shop in the (mall.) For himself, he gets a frozen treat with (walnuts.)

Circle and write the word that best completes each sentence.

1. Walt is not _____ small _____.   (small)   wall   call

2. He has to get pants at the _____ mall _____.   wall   (mall)   hall

3. He plans to get there by _____ walking _____.   (walking)   talking   balking

4. He _____ calls _____ Beth to see if she'll go.   stalls   halls   (calls)

5. He tells her he'll get her a _____ malt _____.   (malt)   salt   walnut

6. They _____ talk _____ about a plan to meet.   (talk)   walk   stall

7. Walt likes the _____ fall _____ breeze.   (fall)   tall   salt

8. He asks for a treat with _____ walnuts _____.   (walnuts)   salt   stalks

Harcourt

Name_____

The Audition

Write a sentence in each box below to help you summarize "The Audition." Be sure to write the events in the correct order.

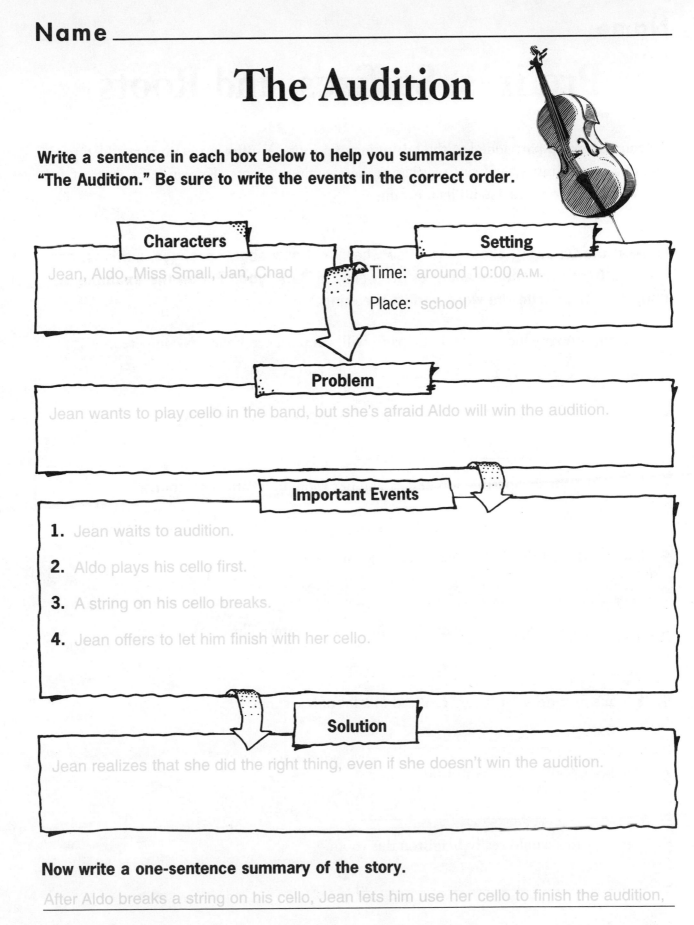

Characters

Jean, Aldo, Miss Small, Jan, Chad

Setting

Time: around 10:00 A.M.

Place: school

Problem

Jean wants to play cello in the band, but she's afraid Aldo will win the audition.

Important Events

1. Jean waits to audition.

2. Aldo plays his cello first.

3. A string on his cello breaks.

4. Jean offers to let him finish with her cello.

Solution

Jean realizes that she did the right thing, even if she doesn't win the audition.

Now write a one-sentence summary of the story.

After Aldo breaks a string on his cello, Jean lets him use her cello to finish the audition, even though it means she may not get a place in the band.

Prefixes, Suffixes, and Roots

A prefix is a word part added to the beginning of a root. A suffix is a word part added to the end of a root. Prefixes and suffixes change the meaning of roots. Knowing the parts of a word can help you understand its meaning.

Look at the following sentences. Use what you know about prefixes, suffixes, and roots to figure out the meaning of the words in dark type. Follow the example in number 1 to rewrite the word and its meaning.

1. It is **unknown** which of the participants will win until everyone has competed.

   un + known = not known

2. Each time Kevin threw the stick, the **playful** puppy brought it back.

   play + ful = full of play

3. Karen had the **impossible** job of cleaning her room in less than an hour.

   im + possible = not possible

4. Laura was **envious** of my success on the test.

   envy + ous = full of envy

5. The movie **preview** promised an exciting new adventure film.

   pre + view = before viewing

6. A bear's **fondness** for honey can lead to a lot of bee stings.

   fond + ness = state of being fond

7. The book Kelly read was **nonfiction**.

   non + fiction = not fiction

8. New curtains would really **brighten** this room.

   bright + en = to make bright

Harcourt

Fluency Builder

ridiculed	**wanted**	**smart**
dignity	**new**	**career**
counsel	**teacher**	**Barbara**
potential	**grandma**	**started**
inspire	**sat**	
correspondence	**she**	
mentor	**talk**	
	with	
	their	

1. Jane's correspondence / with her grandma / was by e-mail.

2. Barbara Jordan was / a smart career woman / with dignity and confidence.

3. Jane's classmates were inspired / by the talk / she gave / on the career / of Barbara Jordan.

4. Barbara Jordan was not ridiculed / by her peers. / They counseled her / to run for the U.S. Congress.

5. Later, / Barbara Jordan started a new career / as a teacher. / She was / a mentor and guide / to her students.

6. Wilma Downs feels / that her granddaughter / has as much potential / as Barbara Jordan.

7. Barbara Jordan wanted / to inspire others / to achieve their potential.

8. The class / liked Jane's talk so much that / she asked her grandma / to talk to the class.

Lessons from Barbara Jordan

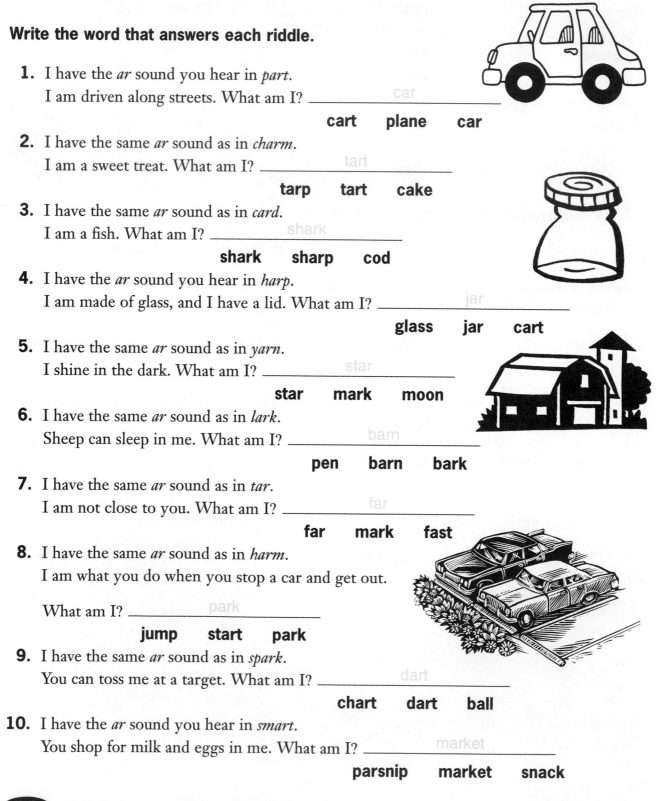

Write the word that answers each riddle.

1. I have the *ar* sound you hear in *part*.
   I am driven along streets. What am I? _____ car

   cart   plane   car

2. I have the same *ar* sound as in *charm*.
   I am a sweet treat. What am I? _____ tart

   tarp   tart   cake

3. I have the same *ar* sound as in *card*.
   I am a fish. What am I? _____ shark

   shark   sharp   cod

4. I have the *ar* sound you hear in *harp*.
   I am made of glass, and I have a lid. What am I? _____ jar

   glass   jar   cart

5. I have the same *ar* sound as in *yarn*.
   I shine in the dark. What am I? _____ star

   star   mark   moon

6. I have the same *ar* sound as in *lark*.
   Sheep can sleep in me. What am I? _____ barn

   pen   barn   bark

7. I have the same *ar* sound as in *tar*.
   I am not close to you. What am I? _____ far

   far   mark   fast

8. I have the same *ar* sound as in *harm*.
   I am what you do when you stop a car and get out.

   What am I? _____ park

   jump   start   park

9. I have the same *ar* sound as in *spark*.
   You can toss me at a target. What am I? _____ dart

   chart   dart   ball

10. I have the *ar* sound you hear in *smart*.
    You shop for milk and eggs in me. What am I? _____ market

    parsnip   market   snack

Harcourt

Lessons from Barbara Jordan

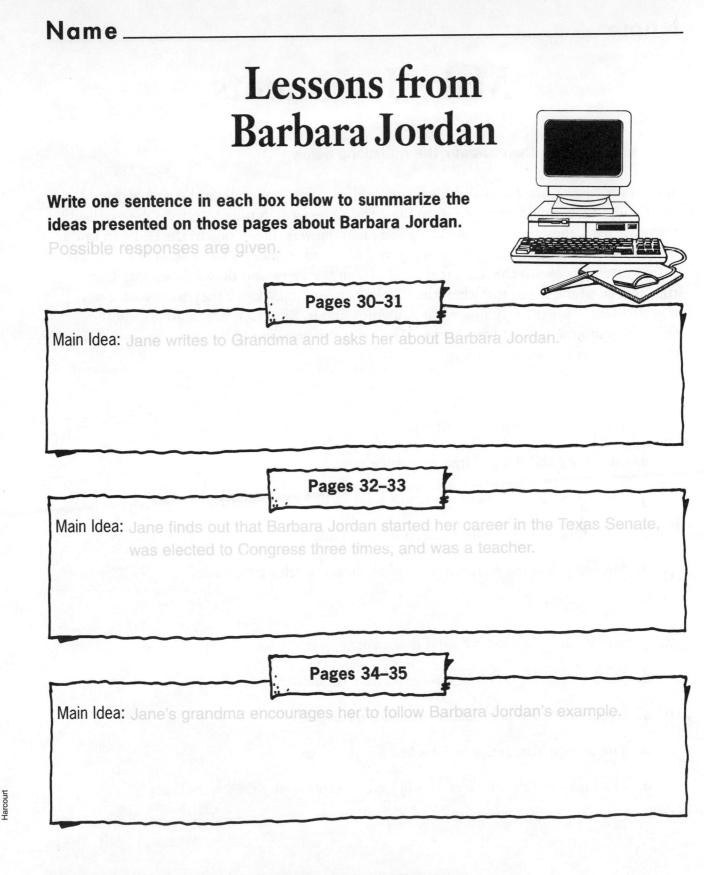

Write one sentence in each box below to summarize the ideas presented on those pages about Barbara Jordan.
Possible responses are given.

Pages 30–31

Main Idea: Jane writes to Grandma and asks her about Barbara Jordan.

Pages 32–33

Main Idea: Jane finds out that Barbara Jordan started her career in the Texas Senate, was elected to Congress three times, and was a teacher.

Pages 34–35

Main Idea: Jane's grandma encourages her to follow Barbara Jordan's example.

Now write a one-sentence summary of the selection.

Jane gets information from her grandmother about Barbara Jordan.

Make Judgments

Read the passage, then answer the questions below.

Just before dinner, Mr. Jones and his three children went for a walk in the woods. Mrs. Jones told them dinner would be ready in an hour and to be back in time to eat. As they walked down the path, they noticed some birds and many flowers. Soon, one of the children saw a fawn. The baby deer could be seen in a grassy area and seemed to be looking at them. They moved carefully toward the deer. It started to scamper away, and they followed it. They soon lost the trail of the fawn, and when they looked around, they knew they were lost. They began to search for the way home but could not find it. By accident, Mr. Jones and the children found the trail and ran home. Mrs. Jones was standing in the doorway with a frown on her face and her arms folded.

1. Which of the following is a valid judgment?

    a. Mr. Jones and the children forgot the time.

    b. Mr. Jones and the children did not want to be late for dinner.

    c. Mr. Jones and the children did not like wildlife.

    d. Mr. Jones and the children felt bad about not catching the fawn.

2. Which of the following is a valid judgment?

    a. Mr. Jones and the children were on time for dinner.

    b. Dinner included cold salads and sandwiches.

    c. The dinner Mrs. Jones had cooked was delicious.

    d. Mr. Jones and the children would have to explain why they were late.

Harcourt

Fluency Builder

revolution	have	paid
plunged	his	that
ravine	found	main
mocking	fine	land
determination	care	paint
condolences	art	sand
	would	
	said	

1. Pablo paid Diego his condolences / when he found out / that Diego had to leave / their fine land / and sail to Mexico.

2. When Diego talked / about how he had to paint their homeland, / Pablo said in a mocking tone, / "They do not care for art there."

3. However, / Diego showed much determination.

4. When he got to Mexico, / he plunged into his job / and painted jungle ravines / filled with vines.

5. Much of Diego's art / spoke of the revolution / of his land.

6. He invited Pablo / to come and see / one of his paintings.

7. Pablo told Diego / that his painting was / a "genuine piece of art."

8. Finally, / Diego's work / was made public, / and everyone grew / to appreciate his art.

Painting My Homeland

**Read the story. Then choose the best answer for each
question. Circle the letter for that answer.**

Clayton looked down the tracks for the midday train. It was always late. As he waited, he
started daydreaming about Spain. He was traveling there next week with his wife, Gail.

"Please," said a man who had a little boy with him, interrupting his daydream, "where
can we catch the train to Main Street?"

"You can stay here with me. I'm catching that train, too," Clayton responded.

"Good," the man said. Then the man spoke to the boy in Spanish.

Clayton said, "Excuse me for asking, but are you from Spain?"

"Yes, I am!" the man said. He looked puzzled.

"Let me explain," Clayton said. "My wife and I are visiting Spain next week. We are very
pleased to be going. The trip is always on my brain!"

The man smiled. "Spain is hot this time of year," he said. "What are your travel plans?"

"We hope to visit some of the historic landmarks, go sailing, and play in the sun. It will
be fantastic!"

1 What was Clayton looking for?
  A the midday bus
  B a cab on Main Street
  C the evening train
  D the midday train

2 What did he do while he waited?
  F He daydreamed about his trip.
  G He clapped his hands.
  H He played a game.
  J He filed his nails.

3 What are Clayton and Gail going to do?
  A wait for rain
  B travel to Spain
  C sail to Paris
  D pay for pancakes

4 The man from Spain
  F started daydreaming, too.
  G asked Clayton about the mail.
  H spoke in Spanish.
  J was afraid of cats.

5 What was the man looking for?
  A a cab to Main Street
  B a bag of grain
  C the train Clayton was waiting for
  D a needle in a haystack

6 Why did Clayton ask the man if he was
  from Spain?
  F He wanted to explain why the train
    was late.
  G The man spoke in Spanish.
  H He wanted to say a joke.
  J The man had paid for his Spanish
    lessons.

Harcourt

Painting My Homeland

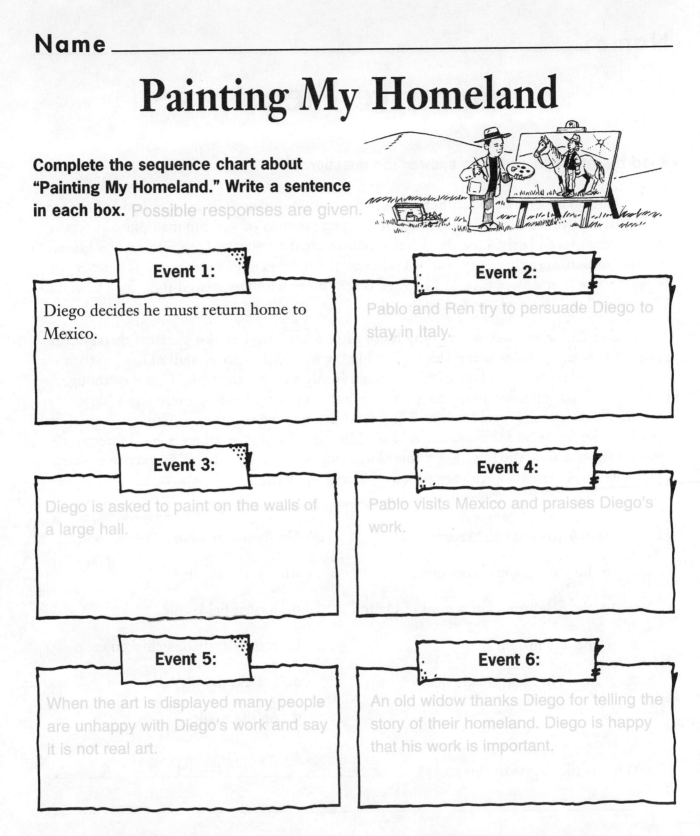

Complete the sequence chart about "Painting My Homeland." Write a sentence in each box. Possible responses are given.

Event 1:

Diego decides he must return home to Mexico.

Event 2:

Pablo and Ren try to persuade Diego to stay in Italy.

Event 3:

Diego is asked to paint on the walls of a large hall.

Event 4:

Pablo visits Mexico and praises Diego's work.

Event 5:

When the art is displayed many people are unhappy with Diego's work and say it is not real art.

Event 6:

An old widow thanks Diego for telling the story of their homeland. Diego is happy that his work is important.

Now use the information from the boxes to write a one-sentence summary of the selection.

Diego Rivera returned to his homeland, where he painted scenes that told of Mexico's people and their history.

Harcourt

Narrative Elements

Read the passage and then answer the questions.

Marty and Ben were brothers who had just moved with their mother and father from New York to live on a farm in Ohio. Each boy liked to help others and made sure games at school were played fairly. One day when a bully started a fight with the pitcher of a game, Marty and Ben were there to break it up before the fighters got in trouble. The pitcher became a fast friend after that. When Fred forgot his lunch, they shared their food with him. They were kind to people and animals alike.

One day when they were going home after school, they took a shortcut through Mr. Blade's fields and past his barns. They didn't know why, but the back wall of the pig barn was so close to the fence that a boy of twelve could barely squeeze through. That day, though, you wouldn't have wanted to try to get through that opening because there was a big sow stuck in there, and she wasn't happy. Marty and Ben worked together to free up some of the boards in the fence, and the sow came loose. She ranted and snorted for a good fifteen minutes. By the time the boys got home, Mr. Blade had called to thank the boys for their help. The boys' parents were very proud of Marty and Ben.

1. As the story begins, the setting is

    a. in the sixth grade classroom.

    b. on the playground at school in Ohio.

    c. in the lunchroom.

    d. at home in New York.

2. On their way home after school, what is the setting?

    a. a corn field

    b. near Mr. Blade's chicken coop

    c. behind the pig barn

    d. on the road

3. What is the theme of this story? __People who are helpful get praise and recognition.__ _____

4. How do the characters' actions help you identify the theme? __Their helpful actions__ __are examples of the kinds of things boys do. The description of their actions__ __helps explain why Mr. Blade calls and why their parents are proud of them.__ _____

Harcourt

Fluency Builder

lineup	ball	down
ace	someone	after
error	that	boast
artificial	would	billboard
control tower	because	groaned
dedicated	star	
	lost	
	hard	
	couldn't	

1. Roberto Clemente / was a dedicated ball player.

2. He promised himself / that he would play hard / for his team.

3. People groaned / that the Pirates / couldn't beat the ace lineup / of the Orioles.

4. The billboard / at the ballpark read / "Home of the Orioles."

5. Clemente, / the star player, / said that was an error. / His team / was going to win!

6. Although he was one / of the best baseball players, / Clemente didn't boast.

7. Clemente gave money to someone / who needed artificial legs.

8. In 1972, / Roberto Clemente lost his life. / The control tower / didn't see / that the plane he rode in / was about to go down.

9. After he lost his life, / Clemente's fans dedicated / a statue to him.

The Pirate Hero

Read the story. Circle all the words that have the short sound of the vowel *o*. Draw a line under all the words that have the long sound of the vowel *o*.

Rob, Kim, and Joan went camping near a lake. Joan steered the boat into the bank with confidence. Rob jumped out and tugged the boat up onto the rocks. "What a mess!" Joan said as she got out. Wind had whipped up the waves on the lake. Her pants legs were wet. Her socks were soaked.

"Let's unload this stuff," Kim said. Rob grabbed the sleeping bags and pitched them up onto the bank. Then he grabbed his rod and reel.

"I'll catch a fine fish!" he boasted. "We can roast it on some coals." Then off he went. Kim moaned. She did not care much for ordinary lake fish. But Joan had said that one must make sacrifices when camping.

"Well, fish it is," Kim said. "I'll put my coat on and get some sticks." Joan helped her. They made a hot blaze. Rob came back in a bit. He held a line of gleaming fish. They roasted the fish on a grate on the coals. They made hot toast to have with it. Then they ate. Kim said with surprise, "This is the best fish I've ever had, Rob! Thanks!"

Now write the long *o* word or the short *o* word that best completes each sentence.

1. _____Joan_____ said that one must make sacrifices when camping.

2. Joan, Rob, and Kim got to the camping spot in a _____boat_____.

3. Joan's pants and _____socks_____ got wet on the trip.

4. Wind-whipped waves had _____soaked_____ her.

5. Rob grabbed his fishing _____rod_____ when they got to the site.

6. He _____boasted_____ that he'd catch some fine fish.

7. Kim _____groaned_____ at the prospect of eating lake fish.

8. They _____roasted_____ the fish.

Harcourt

Name _____

The Pirate Hero

**Complete the sequence chart about "The Pirate Hero." Write a sentence in
each box.** Possible responses are given.

Event 1:

The Pirates lose the first two games to
the Orioles.

Event 2:

Roberto Clemente helps the Pirates win
the third and fourth games.

Event 3:

With Roberto Clemente's help, the
Pirates win the set of games.

Event 4:

In 1972, Roberto Clemente died in a
plane crash on his way to help people.

**Now use the information from the boxes to write a one-sentence summary of
the selection.**

Possible response: Roberto Clemente was a hero in and out of baseball.

_____

_____

Draw Conclusions

Read the paragraph. Then answer the questions below.

Some animals should not be kept together. Max and Rory went to one of their favorite nature areas to find animals. As Max found a green frog near the pond, Rory noticed a warty toad on an old tree stump. They caught the animals and took them home. Rory had a large fish tank, so they placed the toad and the frog in the tank. Instead of putting water in the tank, they left it empty and put a small bowl of water in one corner. They noticed the frog stayed away from the toad but thought that was normal. When the frog didn't move anymore, they took it out of the tank. In a short time, the frog opened its eyes and began to move around. They kept the animals in separate tanks after that.

1. Which is the best conclusion based on the information in the paragraph?

   a. Frogs fall asleep when captured.

   b. Toads may eat frogs.

   c. Toads give off a toxic scent that is poisonous to other animals.

   d. Frogs need water to live.

2. Explain how you came to the conclusion you chose for Question 1.

   Possible response: The paragraph says that after the frog was out of the tank
   it began to move. It sounds as though when it was in the tank it may have been
   sick. I know that some animals protect themselves with special scents. It seems
   that the reason the boys decided to separate the frog and the toad was that
   the toad's scent was dangerous to the frog.

Harcourt

Fluency Builder

diligence	what	grow
plodded	through	rainbow
bountiful	sun	snow
destiny	help	know
assured	rain	slow
entrusted	fine	glow
	grass	
	tree	

1. The Sun rewarded the Rain / for her diligence / with helping the trees / to grow.

2. The people plodded / down the road / covered with snow.

3. The Rain assured the Snow / that the people needed her / to help the grass / to grow.

4. The Rain took credit / for the bountiful harvest / of fine wheat and oats.

5. The Rain and the Snow / entrusted the Sun / with an important decision.

6. At first / the Sun was slow / to take sides. / "I must know / what you can do," / she said.

7. It is the destiny / of both the Rain and the Snow / to be important.

8. The glow / of the Sun / through the rain / made a rainbow.

Harcourt

The Rain and the Snow

Do what the sentences tell you to do.

1. Find three cats in a row. Add a cat to the row.
2. Make a bowl for the cats.
3. Make a tree growing next to the pond.
4. Put a crow up in the tree.
5. Show a leaf blowing away from the tree.
6. Put a dog in the shade below the tree.
7. Put an X on the rowboat next to the pond.
8. A boy named Rob owns the boat. Show who Rob is by making an *R* on his hat.
9. Oh, no, it's snowing! Make some snow falling.
10. Make a pile of six snowballs in Rob's boat.
11. Make Rob hold a paddle to row the boat with.
12. Find the fish. Then make an arrow that shows Rob the way to the pond.
13. Show some of the bubbles the fish are blowing.
14. Find one cat that's not in a row of cats. Make a small bowl for it to eat out of.

Now circle all the words that have the long sound of the vowel *o* spelled *ow*.

Harcourt

The Rain and the Snow

Complete the sequence chart about "The Rain and the Snow."
Possible responses are given.

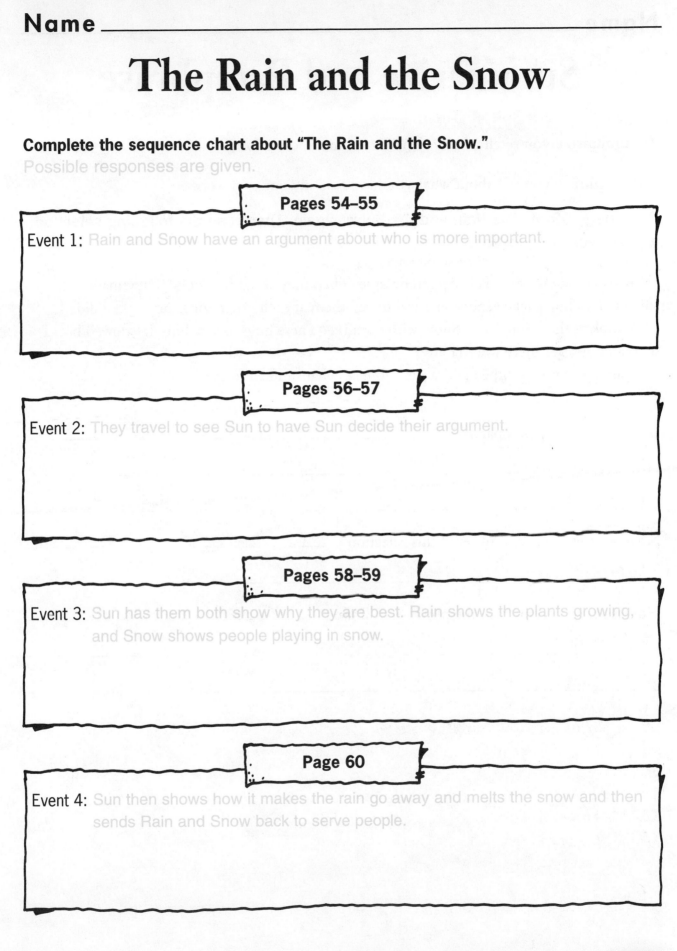

Pages 54–55

Event 1: Rain and Snow have an argument about who is more important.

Pages 56–57

Event 2: They travel to see Sun to have Sun decide their argument.

Pages 58–59

Event 3: Sun has them both show why they are best. Rain shows the plants growing, and Snow shows people playing in snow.

Page 60

Event 4: Sun then shows how it makes the rain go away and melts the snow and then sends Rain and Snow back to serve people.

Summarize and Paraphrase

To **summarize** you retell what you have read in a shorter form.

To **paraphrase** you tell about what you have read in your own words.

Read page 59 of "The Rain and the Snow" again. Then read the following selection and answer the questions.

Kids and moms and dads peered outside. Then they raced outdoors. They made snowmen. They packed snowballs and tossed them at each other, giggling as they did.

"Look at that, Sun," said Snow with a smirk. "These guys love rolling in snow. They'd be really upset if there weren't any."

Rain and Snow stopped and waited to hear what sun had to say.

Is this a summary or a paraphrase? _paraphrase_____

How do you know? _It is a retelling of the selection that is similar length but uses_

_different words._____

Now use the other skill to retell this selection. _Possible response: Snow shows how_

much people like snow and then Rain and Snow wait for Sun's wise answer.

How is this different from the previous skill used? _Possible response: This summary_

differs from the paraphrase because it includes only important details and

is much shorter.

Fluency Builder

headquarters
positions
handlers
tangle
pace

was
were
step
out
along
help
dog
early
after
from
couldn't

snowstorm
morning
door
transporting

1. The medical headquarters / was located / in Anchorage, Alaska.

2. The obstacles / to transporting the medicine / were incredible.

3. Day after day, / the medicine traveled nonstop, / passing from one musher / to the next.

4. When a snowstorm hit, / the huskies couldn't keep pace.

5. They stepped out of their positions / and tangled their lines.

6. There were no extra dog handlers / along to help.

7. In the early morning darkness, / Dr. Welch heard a rap / at his door.

8. The race for life / was won.

Race for Life on the Iditarod Trail

Circle and write the word that makes sense in the sentence.

1. Dogsledding is a hard and demanding _____.

   sport

   spot   (sport)   spoke

2. Sled drivers, called mushers, must travel in bad _____.

   storms

   (storms)   stoves   stomps

3. Huskies are _____ to the job of pulling sleds.

   born

   barn   (born)   bond

4. On the trail, sled dogs sleep in

   _____ made of snow.

   forts

   farms   forests   (forts)

5. Thick coats help the dogs sleep well on a _____ made
   of snow.

   floor

   (floor)   flute   flock

6. A lot of sled dog breeders make their homes in the far _____.

   north

   (north)   nor   not

7. The musher must keep _____ within the team of dogs.

   order

   odder   (order)   orchard

8. A musher must have a job _____ each dog and must teach the
   dog to do it well.

   for

   fort   far   (for)

9. A mush team's day often starts early in

   the _____.

   morning

   moon   mound   (morning)

10. But sled dogs do an _____ job, and they like the job
    they do.

    important

    (important)   impostor   immortal

11. The people of Nome, Alaska, will never _____ how dogsled
    teams saved lives one winter.

    forget

    (forget)   forlorn   forts

Harcourt

Name_____

Race for Life on the Iditarod Trail

Complete the sequence chart about "Race for Life on the Iditarod Trail." Write a sentence in each box.

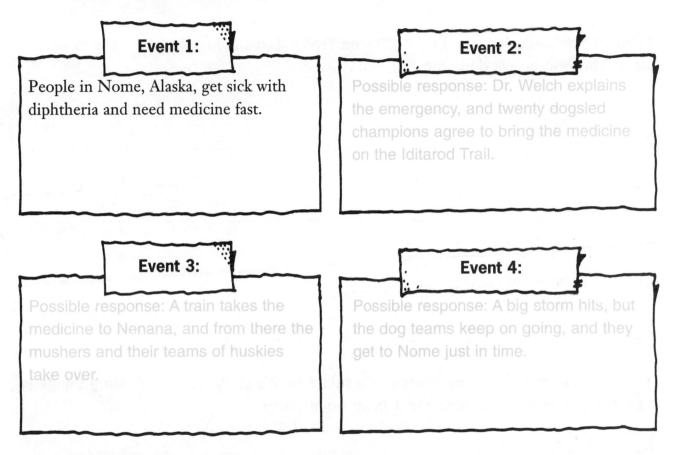

Event 1:

People in Nome, Alaska, get sick with diphtheria and need medicine fast.

Event 2:

Possible response: Dr. Welch explains the emergency, and twenty dogsled champions agree to bring the medicine on the Iditarod Trail.

Event 3:

Possible response: A train takes the medicine to Nenana, and from there the mushers and their teams of huskies take over.

Event 4:

Possible response: A big storm hits, but the dog teams keep on going, and they get to Nome just in time.

Now use the information from the boxes to write a one-sentence summary of the entire selection.

Possible response: The people of Nome are saved from diphtheria when dogsled teams travel the Iditarod Trail to bring them medicine.

Harcourt

Draw Conclusions

Fill in the blanks.

To **draw conclusions** about a selection, you need to notice the story details and draw from your own experience.

Think about "Race for Life on the Iditarod Trail." List the important details of the story. The first one is done for you. Possible responses are given.

1. Children have diphtheria.

2. The medicine is far away.

3. Because of the weather, dogsleds are the only way to get there.

4. Champion dogsledders take on the task.

5. They work like a relay team, never stopping.

6. The weather gets worse and slows them down.

7. They get the medicine there in time.

Now list your personal experiences that relate to this story. Focus on doing things in bad weather and how people react in an emergency.

1. Responses will vary.

2. _____

3. _____

What conclusions can you draw about the people in this story?

1. These mushers are able to work very hard, because they are champions.

2. Answers will vary.

Harcourt

Fluency Builder

resembled	watch	adore
retired	over	four
snort	family	oars
harness	fish	bore
disengage	made	chore
bulk	from	wore
pointedly		roar

1. The rhythm of the oars / bore them / over the waves.

2. Fishing isn't a chore / for the four family members.

3. Little Elinore / wore her harness / over her life jacket's bulk.

4. Suze said pointedly, / "I'm going to catch more fish / than you!"

5. When dad disengaged the motor, / it made a snort / and went still.

6. One more wiggling fish / had retired from swimming.

7. The fish resembled / a little man with long whiskers.

8. I watched the sun set / over the sea / we adore.

Fishing for Four

Read the story. Circle all the words that have the vowel sound heard in *more*.

Norm, the chimp, had lots of chores to do. He had to feed his pet boar. He had to cut some boards to fix the boar's pen. He had to stack the oars in the shed. Then there were ripe gourds to pick and store in the attic. "I'm bored with this routine," Norm complained. "What will it matter if I skip the chores just one time?" Norm went up to his bed. He started to snore. Meanwhile, the hungry boar left its pen to explore. When Norm woke up, he stared in disbelief! What a mess! The boar had gobbled up all the gourds. It had run over the oars and smashed them to bits. "What more?" Norm wailed as he ran to the shed. The boar was there, munching on apple cores. There were no more apples in the bin.

Circle and write the word that best completes each sentence.

1. Norm skipped his ____chores____.   **store**   **boar**   **chores**

2. His pet ____boar____ got out of its pen.   **gourd**   **goat**   **boar**

3. Norm's mistake was in getting ____bored____.   **bored**   **poured**   **sore**

4. He was supposed to pick the ____gourds____.   **corn**   **gourds**   **cores**

5. He was supposed to stack the ____oars____.   **cores**   **gourds**   **oars**

6. He was supposed to cut the ____boards____.   **more**   **boards**   **corn**

7. It was not smart of Norm to ____snore____ all day.   **snore**   **core**   **soar**

8. Now he has a bigger job than he had ____before____.   **implore**   **before**   **ignore**

Fishing for Four

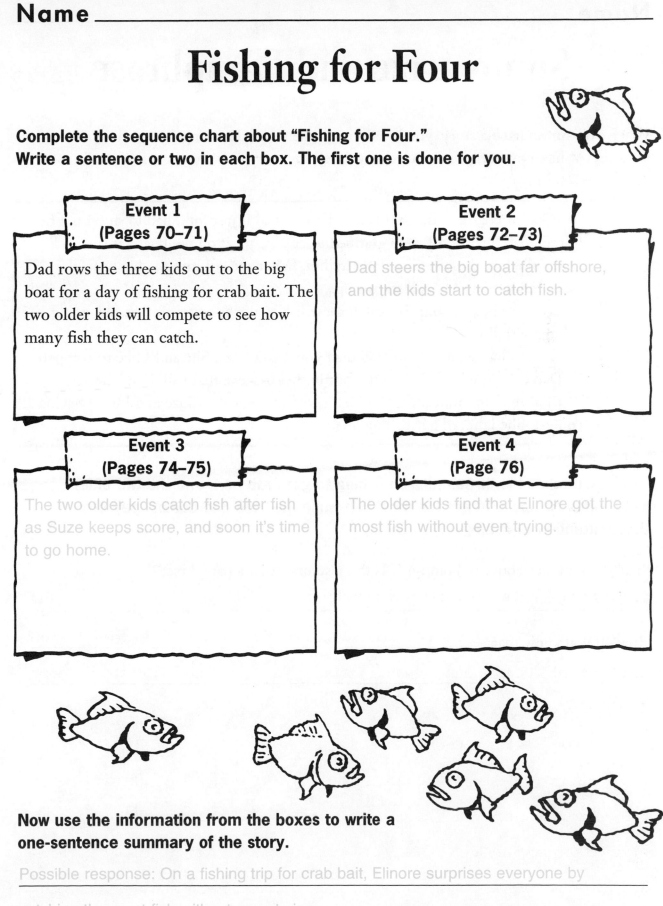

Complete the sequence chart about "Fishing for Four."
Write a sentence or two in each box. The first one is done for you.

Event 1
(Pages 70–71)

Dad rows the three kids out to the big boat for a day of fishing for crab bait. The two older kids will compete to see how many fish they can catch.

Event 2
(Pages 72–73)

Dad steers the big boat far offshore, and the kids start to catch fish.

Event 3
(Pages 74–75)

The two older kids catch fish after fish as Suze keeps score, and soon it's time to go home.

Event 4
(Page 76)

The older kids find that Elinore got the most fish without even trying.

Now use the information from the boxes to write a one-sentence summary of the story.

Possible response: On a fishing trip for crab bait, Elinore surprises everyone by

catching the most fish without even trying.

Harcourt

Summarize and Paraphrase

When you **summarize** a story, you briefly retell the main idea using facts and details from the story. When you **paraphrase** a story, you tell the story, but use your own words.

"Get on board, kids," said Dad. Elinore, who is just four, had to sit on the floor of the boat. Suze and I were gratified to be able to sit on the board at the back. Dad pulled on the oars in a slow rhythm. When we got into the big boat, the motor emitted a roar as it started up.

We were helping our dad catch some fish to use as crab bait. We like going fishing with him.

"I'm going to catch more fish than you," said Suze. She and I like to compete. Dad calculated. "If we can fill four bushel baskets, that will do it," he said.

Elinore is an innocent little kid. She didn't know that Suze and I were having a contest. She ignored her fishing line.

Dad takes his three children fishing to get crab bait, and the two older ones compete to get the most fish while the little one doesn't pay any attention to fishing.

Read the sentence above in bold type. Is this a summary or a paraphrase?

It is a summary.
_____

How do you know that? _A summary tells only the most important ideas, and is_

usually much shorter than the original passage.
_____

Harcourt

Fluency Builder

overcome   away   worked
forlorn   could   fur
pitched   watch   churning
vainer   over   search
gorged   lost   turned
abalone   without   gurgling
lair   knew

1. Lani could not go / with the men / to search / for abalone.

2. She felt lost and forlorn / as she watched / the men paddle away.

3. Kalo said / that Lani could hide in his canoe, / and she was overcome / with joy.

4. Kalo and Lani passed / by the lair / of the seals / and watched a vainer seal / lick his fur all over.

5. The other seals / gorged themselves / on fish.

6. Suddenly, / a fierce storm / turned over the canoes / of the other men.

7. Lani and Kalo worked together / to paddle through / the churning water / and turn over the flipped canoes.

8. All of the men knew / they would have been lost / in the gurgling waves / without Lani's help.

Name _____

Raindrop in the Sun

Write the word that answers each riddle.

1. I have the same vowel sound and spelling as in *pearl*.

   I am a planet. What am I? _____Earth_____

   Earth   earn   Saturn

2. I have the same vowel sound and spelling as in *turn*.

   I am a color. What am I? _____purple_____

   purse   purple   teal

3. I have the same vowel sound and spelling as in *bird*.

   Girls dress up in me. What am I? _____skirt_____

   twirl   dress   skirt

4. I have the same vowel sound and spelling as in *herd*.

   I am a kind of fish. What am I? _____perch_____

   perch   search   fern

5. I have the same vowel sound and spelling as in *work*.

   I mean the opposite of better. What am I? _____worse_____

   woods   worms   worse

6. I have the same vowel sound and spelling as in the first syllable of *early*.

   I mean "to have an earnest desire." What am I? _____yearn_____

   yearn   hope   learn

7. I have the same vowel sound and spelling as in *burn*.

   I mean "silly or senseless." What am I? _____absurd_____

   turned   absurd   odd

8. I have the same vowel sound and spelling as in *dirt*.

   I am a kind of tree. What am I? _____birch_____

   birch   maple   shirt

Harcourt

Raindrop in the Sun

Complete the chart to retell the story.

Cause		**Effect**
Moro told Lani she was too weak to paddle a ___canoe___. **raft canoe rowboat**	⇨	Kalo told Lani to meet him by the cave's ___entrance___. He hid her in his boat. **entrance side back**
Kalo and Lani ___worked___ well as a team. **worked played hid**	⇨	Kalo and Lani ___gathered___ a lot of abalones. **cleaned ate gathered**
A ___fierce___ storm came up. Lani and Kalo saved the men. **soft fierce winter**	⇨	Moro ___strode___ up and gave a speech. He called Lani a hero. **drove flew strode**

Now write a sentence that summarizes the story.

Possible response: Lani is told she is not strong enough to help gather abalones, but she later proves to be a valuable member of her tribe.

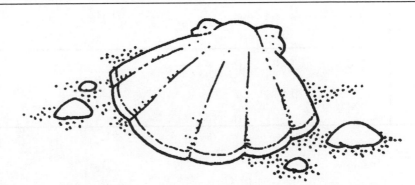

Harcourt

Narrative Elements

Read the story. Fill in the Narrative Elements chart below with information from the story.

Mr. and Mrs. Sanson took their family to the beach. They had two sons: Bret, a fifth grader, and Kirk, a first grader. After they found a good spot, they put down their blankets and set up an umbrella. It wasn't long before Kirk started to build sand houses and roads for his metal cars to drive on. He brought three of his favorite cars to the beach. Bret seemed interested in electricity and magnetism and brought a few books to read. At noon the family had lunch, and afterward, when Kirk returned to his sand houses and cars, they were not there. Someone must have driven over them by accident. He searched with his hands and found one car. When his family saw what had happened, Bret remembered he had a horseshoe magnet in the car. He got it, and Kirk and Bret used it to find the cars in the sand.

NARRATIVE ELEMENTS

Characters	Mr. Sanson, Mrs. Sanson, Bret and Kirk
Setting	the beach
Plot: Problem or Conflict	Kirk leaves his toy cars in the sand. When he returns the cars are gone.
Plot: Solution	Kirk finds one of the cars by digging around in the sand. Bret uses a magnet to find the other metal cars in the sand.
Theme	Possible response: Bret's interest in science comes in useful at a family outing at the beach.

Harcourt

Fluency Builder

eons	birthday	both
peninsula	his	over
scurried	will	we
multitude	started	find
plenitude	help	Jason
pondered	change	ago
	were	become

1. Eons ago / manatees scurried / over the land / like other mammals.

2. There were a multitude / of manatees /on both sides / of the Florida peninsula.

3. Manatees help / keep the plenitude / of weeds / from choking Florida waterways.

4. Jason pondered / the manatee model / his grandpa gave him / for a birthday gift.

5. Jason wanted to help change / the fate faced / by manatees.

6. Over time / manatees will become extinct / if we don't help them.

7. If everyone started to help, / then multitudes / of manatees would always swim / in Florida waterways.

8. Jason plans / to find a club / on the Web / or start one / of his own.

Name_____

The Gift of the Manatee

Circle the letter in front of the sentence that tells about the picture.

1 A Willy pets the lion.
   B Willy stands behind the zebra.
   C Willy uses the broom.
   D Willy rolls under the zebra.

2 F April hides the tomatoes in her apron.
   G April stirs the tomatoes with a ladle.
   H April holds the tomatoes in the crate.
   J April picks the tomatoes from her home.

3 A Emily is a pilot in the Navy.
   B Emily cares for lions at the wildlife park.
   C Emily explores volcanoes.
   D Emily has a program on the radio.

4 F Ruby's baby sister finds a tiny radio.
   G Ruby's baby sister rides an old bike.
   H Ruby's baby sister winds the funny clock.
   J Ruby's baby sister finds an acorn.

5 A Ty and Mona dry their hands on their aprons.
   B Ty and Mona don't like the flavor of tuna.
   C Ty and Mona try to keep dry in the rain.
   D Ty and Mona think the lake is cold.

6 F Peter makes the ball fly over the goal posts.
   G Peter finds a spider behind the piano.
   H Peter grinds the corn with a stone.
   J Peter strolls by the cargo door.

Harcourt

The Gift of the Manatee

Write one sentence in each box below to show what you learned about the manatee.

Pages 86–87

What does Jason learn about where the manatee lives, and where it may be going?

Possible response: The manatee lives in warm waters in Florida but is in danger of extinction.

Page 88

How did manatees become water animals?

Possible response: They used to live on land but were forced into the sea, where they developed flippers and tails and learned to eat plants growing in waterways.

Pages 90–91

What does Jason learn about the dangers to the manatee, and what does he decide to do about that?

Possible response: After Jason learns that people are endangering the manatee, he wants to join a save-the-manatee club and get others involved.

Now use the information in the boxes to write a one-sentence summary of the selection.

Possible response: Jason learns that the manatee in Florida is endangered and decides he wants to help.

Prefixes, Suffixes, and Roots

Fill in the blanks to tell about prefixes, suffixes, and roots.

The _____root_____ of a word carries the word's basic meaning.

A _____prefix_____ is added to the beginning of a word.

A _____suffix_____ is added to the end of a word.

Both _____prefixes_____ and _____suffixes_____ change the meaning of the root or root word.

Read the chart. Study the word parts and their meanings. Then answer the questions below.

Prefix		Root		Suffix	
in-	"not"	vis	"see"	-ible	"able"
		aud	"hear"	-ation	"the act of"
		dict	"speak"		

What is the root in the word <u>visible</u>? ___vis___

What is the meaning of the word <u>visible</u>? ___"able to be seen"___

How is the word <u>audible</u> like the word <u>visible</u>? ___They have the same suffix.___

What is the meaning of the word <u>audible</u>? What is the meaning of the word <u>inaudible</u>?

___"able to be heard"; "not able to be heard"___

What is <u>dictation</u>? ___the act of speaking or reading aloud.___

Use the word parts in the chart to form words that you know, and write them on the lines. Then write the meanings of the words. Possible responses are shown.

___dictionary___ _____

___visual___ _____

___informal___ _____

Harcourt

Fluency Builder

Name _____

dwindled
tinder
policy
canopy
embers
geyser
veered

in
park
fire
went
fell
snow
rain
many

showers
spout
ground
however
out

1. Geysers spout / at Yellowstone National Park.

2. In 1988 / Yellowstone became / as dry as tinder.

3. It is the park's policy / to let fires burn / until rain showers end them.

4. Fierce winds / made the fires veer / this way and that.

5. The forest canopy / went up in flames.

6. Red-hot embers / fell to the ground / and started more fires.

7. In September, / snow and rain / caused the flames to dwindle / and finally go out.

8. Through the winter, / the land did not offer much to eat, / however, / many animals survived.

Flowers After the Flames

Read the story, and circle all the words with the same vowel sound as in *pound* and *now*.

Last summer a traveling carnival came to town. For several days, we heard the pounding of hammers and the humming of drills.

A big crowd came to it the first day. Inside the grounds the visitors found lots of rides and games. There was a Ferris wheel that went around and around. There was a winding slide connected to a big tower.

Every hour a parade would wind its way around the grounds. It was led by a grouchy clown mounted on a purple cow. The clown's lips were painted into a big red frown and she wore a funny gown. Just behind her strolled a big round sow. Behind the sow was a growling hound. In the middle of the parade, the hound bounded past the sow. He jumped and landed on the clown, making her fall off the cow. The clown groaned out loud. Everyone in the crowd clapped and cheered.

Now write the word with the same vowel sound as in *pound* and *now* that best completes each sentence.

1. The carnival came to _____town_____ last summer.

2. The slide was connected to a _____tower_____.

3. The first day a big _____crowd_____ attended the carnival.

4. Every hour a parade wound its way _____around_____ the grounds.

5. A _____grouchy_____ clown led the parade.

6. The clown wore a funny gown and had a big red _____frown_____.

7. A sow and a _____hound_____ were behind her.

8. The hound made the clown fall off a purple _____cow_____.

Harcourt

Flowers After the Flames

Write one sentence in each box below to summarize the main idea presented on the given pages. Possible responses are given.

Pages 94–95

Main Idea: In the summer of 1988, dry conditions caused fires at Yellowstone National Park to spread out of control.

Pages 96–97

Main Idea: When snow and rain finally put out the fires, the plants and animals found new ways to survive.

Pages 98–99

Main Idea: Throughout the spring season, new life returned to Yellowstone.

Now write a one-sentence summary of "Flowers After the Flames."

Possible response: Forest fires at Yellowstone National Park made way for new life.

Harcourt

Name _____

Graphic Aids

Graphic aids that are used in books and newspapers include photographs, charts, diagrams, illustrations and maps. Graphic aids can help one understand information that is difficult or complex.

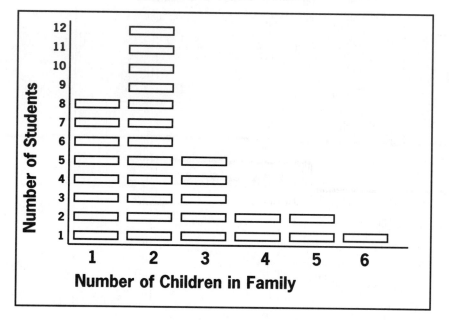

Look at the chart carefully. Then answer these questions.

How many students come from families with exactly two children in them?

_____ 12 _____

How many students come from families with only one child? _____ 8 _____

Two students have families with exactly _____ 4 _____ children, and two

have families with exactly _____ 5 _____ children.

There are only five students with exactly _____ 3 _____ children in the family.

How many students are in this group? _____ 30 _____

Harcourt

Fluency Builder

gravitational	tree	brighter
bulge	bird	sunlight
inlet	this	high
generated	hot	mighty
energy	over	night
shallow	fall	
	had	
	pull	
	come	

1. Krakatoa / was a peaceful place / with many birds, / trees, / and sunlight.

2. Then in 1883, / hot ash from Krakatoa / formed dark clouds / over the ocean, / turning daytime to night.

3. The red glow / over the volcano / grew brighter. / The ocean began / to rise and fall, / smashing the boats / in the inlet.

4. Earthquakes underwater / had generated a tsunami!

5. The tsunami didn't come / from the tidal bulge / made by the gravitational pull / of the moon.

6. It was powered / by the energy / of the earthquakes / started by the explosion / of Krakatoa.

7. The next day, / a new tsunami grew bigger and bigger / as it crossed the shallow waters / near the coastline.

8. The mighty wave / traveled around the world, / and even to this day, / people will never forget / that Krakatoa caused this to happen.

Name _____

The Krakatoa Wave

Do what the sentences tell you to do.

1. It is nighttime. Make the skies dark.
2. Inside, Dwight tries to fix his bike seat. Add a seat to his bike.
3. Dwight's sight is not good. Give him glasses so he can do his work.
4. Dwight must put a bright reflector on the seat of his bike. Put the round reflector in his hand.
5. Dwight has put the bike light on backward. Cross out the light, and sketch it the right way.
6. It is not very bright in here. Add a new light bulb.
7. Mom tries to reach a box, but it is too high. Make a ladder for her.
8. She will need a flashlight to see inside the box. Give her one.
9. Dad has pried open a sealed box. Sketch what is inside.
10. Dad's shoelace has come untied. Draw an untied shoelace on his right shoe.
11. Flick, the cat, cries for a toy. Make a tennis ball for Flick to play with.
12. Flick is missing his spots! Add spots on his thighs and back.
13. Flick likes to lie on rugs. Make a rug for Flick to lie on.
14. Flick is frightened by a bee that flies by. Draw the bee.

Now circle all the words that have the /ī/ sound spelled *igh* or *ie*.

Harcourt

Name_____

The Krakatoa Wave

Complete the sequence chart about "The Krakatoa Wave." Write a sentence in each box. The first one is done for you.

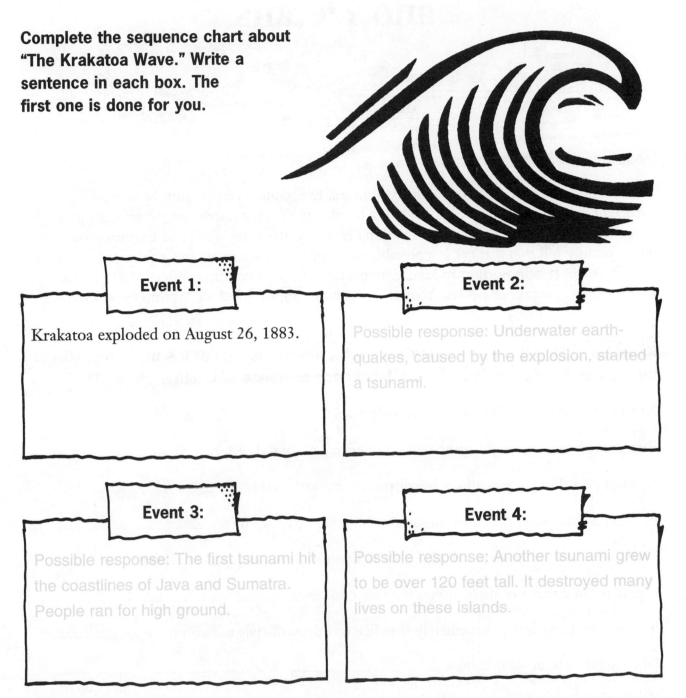

Event 1:

Krakatoa exploded on August 26, 1883.

Event 2:

Possible response: Underwater earthquakes, caused by the explosion, started a tsunami.

Event 3:

Possible response: The first tsunami hit the coastlines of Java and Sumatra. People ran for high ground.

Event 4:

Possible response: Another tsunami grew to be over 120 feet tall. It destroyed many lives on these islands.

Now use the information from the boxes to write a one-sentence summary of the selection.

Possible response: Tsunamis caused by the explosion of Krakatoa in 1883 killed many people on the islands of Java and Sumatra.

Harcourt

Text Structure: Main Idea and Details

Read this paragraph.

Not too many people live near active volcanoes. Everyone, however, might some day experience a natural disaster. It could be a flood, a tornado, a hurricane, or an earthquake. In order to stay safe, the most important thing is to pay attention. Radio or television reports will probably tell you if there is a possible disaster. If you are in an area of danger, you may have to leave. It is important to leave immediately if police or other officials tell you to. Don't worry about your things. Your safety is more important than anything you own.

Read the paragraph again. Decide if each sentence is part of the main idea (MI) or the supporting details (SD). Below, label each sentence with either MI or SD.

Not too many people live near active volcanoes. _____ SD

Everyone, however, might some day experience a natural disaster. _____ MI

It could be a flood, a tornado, a hurricane, or an earthquake. _____ SD

In order to stay safe, the most important thing is to pay attention. _____ SD

Radio or television reports will probably tell you if there is a possible disaster. _____ SD

If you are in an area of danger, you may have to leave. _____ SD

It is important to leave immediately if police or other officials tell you to. _____ SD

Don't worry about your things. _____ SD

Your safety is more important than anything you own. _____ MI

Write the main idea of this paragraph in your own words.

If you are in a disaster, do what you are told and don't worry about your things.

Harcourt

Fluency Builder

sensors	found	edge
reef	around	ridges
lagoon	animal	gently
atoll	grow	largest
barren	between	
meander	floor	
	when	
	sea	
	years	
	without	

1. Coral reefs are found / in oceans / around the world.

2. Each tube-shaped coral animal / has a mouth / surrounded by fingerlike sensors.

3. Some reefs grow / around the edge / of a volcanic island.

4. When water flows / between an ancient volcano / in the ocean floor and a reef, / a calm lagoon is formed.

5. An atoll is created / when the ancient volcano disappears.

6. Sea animals meander / in and out of coral gardens / in the Great Barrier Reef, / the largest on Earth.

7. A coral reef grows very slowly— / its ridges may be only 3 feet higher in 1,000 years.

8. Without sunlight / and gently moving water, / coral reefs would become / barren piles of rock.

Harcourt

Name _____

Gardens of the Sea: Coral Reefs

Read the story. Circle all the words that have the sound the letter g stands for in the word *general*.

The giant giraffe wanted to drink some water. She walked slowly to the edge of the lake.

At the same time, a villager crossed the bridge. He wanted to fill his large bucket with water for his vegetables.

Neither the giraffe nor the villager saw the danger lurking in the hedges. Then a strange sound made them both look up.

A huge cat came flying out of the hedge. It was the largest beast the villager had ever seen. The villager flew like a gymnast into a tree. The giraffe turned and ran over the ridge.

Luckily, wildlife biologists also heard the sound. They trapped the cat in a cage. Then they drove it far away from the village and the lake.

Circle and write the word that best completes each sentence.

1. The giant _____giraffe_____ was thirsty.

   giraffe   **gerbil**   **hedgehog**

2. A villager needed water for his ____vegetables____.

   vegetables   **pages**   **fringe**

3. A huge cat was hiding behind the ____hedge____.

   hedge   **slug**   **ginger**

4. Neither the giraffe nor the man saw the ____danger____.

   gem   **engine**   **danger**

5. Some wildlife ____biologists____ trapped the cat in a cage.

   geologists   **biologists**   **badges**

Harcourt

Gardens of the Sea: Coral Reefs

Write one or two sentences in each box below to show what you learned about coral reefs in "Gardens of the Sea: Coral Reefs."

Pages 110–112

Main Ideas: Possible response: Coral reefs are found in the warmest oceans all around the world. They are formed by the skeletons of small sea animals.

Pages 113–114

Main Ideas: Possible response: There are three kinds of reefs: fringing reefs, barrier reefs, and coral atolls. The Great Barrier Reef is the largest reef on Earth.

Pages 115–116

Main Ideas: Possible response: Sea horses, sea turtles, sea stars, giant clams, and colorful fish live in and around reefs. We must prevent pollution from destroying the reefs.

Write a one-sentence summary statement about the selection.

Possible response: Coral reefs are beautiful undersea gardens full of life that we must care for and preserve.

Graphic Aids

Read the passsage and study the diagram to answer the questions.

Mud, clay, sand, pebbles, and the shells of sea animals are carried to the ocean where they form layers of sediment. The layers of sediment that continue to form create pressure on the layers below to form rock. As more layers of sediment are formed, the rocks near the bottom press together even more and become harder. Sometimes heat within the Earth may change the rocks, too. For example, mud compresses to form a rock called shale. Under more pressure and heat, the shale becomes slate.

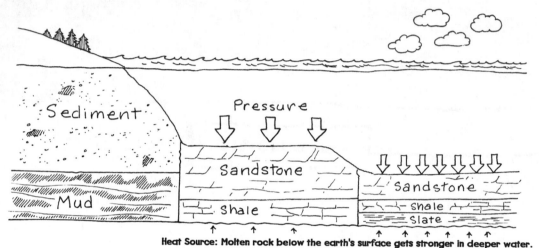

Heat Source: Molten rock below the earth's surface gets stronger in deeper water.

1. Which information in the illustration does the reading selection describe?

   a. Sea animals are pressed together to make limestone.

   b. As shale experiences more pressure, it becomes slate.

   c. Sandstone becomes a hard rock called quartz.

   d. Marble was once the skeletal remains of animals.

2. Which of these does the diagram explain?

   a. The layers of rock are changing due to pressure and heat.

   b. The sea animals live to be hundreds of years old.

   c. Some sand and mud can be carried to the ocean by the wind.

   d. Waves wash against the rocks and slowly break the rock into sand.

Harcourt

Fluency Builder

translation	made	space
publicity	paper	center
features	they	face
piercing	hungry	sincere
advanced	knew	slices
	looks	celery
	their	pencil
	few	

1. The space people advanced / on Miss Clancy / with piercing looks.

2. Miss Clancy made herself / calmly face them / in the center / of the gym.

3. She asked / if they wanted publicity / about their arrival.

4. The space people shook / their heads no, / and they seemed sincere.

5. From their features, / Vince knew / they were from Mars.

6. With paper and pencil, / they made marks / which looked / like a code.

7. After a few minutes, / Vince was able / to make a translation / of the markings.

8. The hungry space people / ate cheese slices / and celery sticks.

Name _____

An Encounter with Space People

Circle and write the word that best completes each sentence.

1. Cathy is teaching Cyrus how to tap _____.

   (**dance**)   **date**   **dark**

2. Cathy has taken tap classes _____ she was six.

   skill   (**since**)   **silence**

3. Cyrus _____ to learn how to dance, too.

   decoded   (**decided**)   **deduced**

4. Cathy and Cyrus stand in the _____ of the hall. They wait for
   the music to begin.   (**center**)   **circle**   **cabin**

5. They spin in _____ as they dance.

   collars   **processes**   (**circles**)

6. Cathy hopes to perform with Cyrus at the winter _____.

   center   (**concert**)   **crowd**

7. She circles the date in _____ on her calendar.

   (**pencil**)   **purple**   **puzzle**

8. On the big night, Cyrus and Cathy both wear _____ costumes.

   (**fancy**)   **finally**   **finicky**

9. When the dancing _____,

   causes   **calls**   (**ceases**)

   the people clap wildly.

10. After the concert, Cathy and Cyrus

    _____ their success.

    celery   **career**   (**celebrate**)

Harcourt

Name _____

An Encounter with Space People

Complete the story map for "An Encounter with Space People."

Characters:

Miss Clancy

Vince

2 space people

Setting:

School classroom.

Events

Space people land in a schoolyard.

They use a secret code to communicate.

One student, Vince, is able to crack the code.

The class gives the space people food and they go on their way.

Name _____

Text Structure: Main Idea and Details

Read the passage. Then answer the question and complete this outline based on the passage.

Native Americans in North America

When European explorers first came to North America, they found people already living there. Those who lived in the woodland areas hunted in the forests and made their homes out of wood and animal hides. They made many tools and clothing from the woodland animals. Those people who lived on the plains hunted buffalo and used the parts of the buffalo for almost everything they had, including their tepees, tools, and weapons. In the southwestern regions, people farmed the land and built their homes of clay since there were no trees or buffalo there. Many native people who lived along the Pacific Coast built their homes of wood and fished in the ocean for much of their food.

What is the implied or suggested idea of this passage? People depended on the land around them for food, clothing, and shelter.

I. People in woodland areas

   A. Possible response: hunted in the forest

   B. Possible response: made homes out of wood and animal hides

II. People in the Plains

   A. hunted buffalo

   B. used the parts of the buffalo for their tepees, tools and weapons

III. People in the southwest

   A. farmed the land

   B. built homes of clay

IV. People along the Pacific Coast

   A. built homes of wood

   B. fished in the ocean for food

Harcourt

Fluency Builder

rations	their	Roy
homestead	step	choice
concocted	was	boil
perch	have	boy
undeniable	when	enjoy
despair	get	
	make	
	pan	
	you're	

1. From their perch / on the porch steps, / Roy and Pearl looked / at the homestead.

2. It was Granny's birthday party / and they planned to have / an exciting weekend.

3. Much to their despair, / Roy and Pearl didn't have / a birthday gift for Granny!

4. Pearl suggested they make / a tasty pan of fudge.

5. Roy said, / "Good choice, / but you're looking / at a boy / who can't even boil water."

6. Roy brooded / about one undeniable fact; / they still had no present for Granny.

7. When Granny tasted the fudge / they had concocted, / they smiled.

8. When Granny was a girl, / sugar rations were precious, / and she didn't get to enjoy sweets / as often as she did now.

Harcourt

Peppermint-Peanut-Butter Fudge

Write the word that answers each riddle.

1. I have the same vowel sound as in *boy*.

   You put me in a car's motor. What am I? _____ oil _____

           oil   gas   owl

2. I have the same vowel sound as in *toy*.

   I live in the sea. What am I? _____ oyster _____

       flounder   oyster   employee

3. I have the same vowel sound as in *joy*.

   You can pay for things with me. What am I? _____ coin _____

       coin   dollar   coil

4. I have the same vowel sound as in *boil*.

   You use me to speak. What am I? _____ voice _____

       choice   voice   mouth

5. My second syllable has the same vowel sound as in *loyal*.

   I am someone's boss. What am I? _____ employer _____

       enjoying   foreman   employer

6. I have the same vowel sound as in *join*.

   I am often loud. What am I? _____ noise _____

       sound   noise   poise

7. My first syllable has the same vowel sound as in *moist*.

   I am a king or queen. What am I? _____ royalty _____

       royalty   loyalty   ruler

8. I have the same vowel sound as in *boys*.

   You can plant seeds in me. What am I? _____ soil _____

       ground   soil   foil

9. My second syllable has the same vowel sound as in *broil*.

   I mean "to bother." What word am I? _____ annoy _____

       appoint   annoy   distract

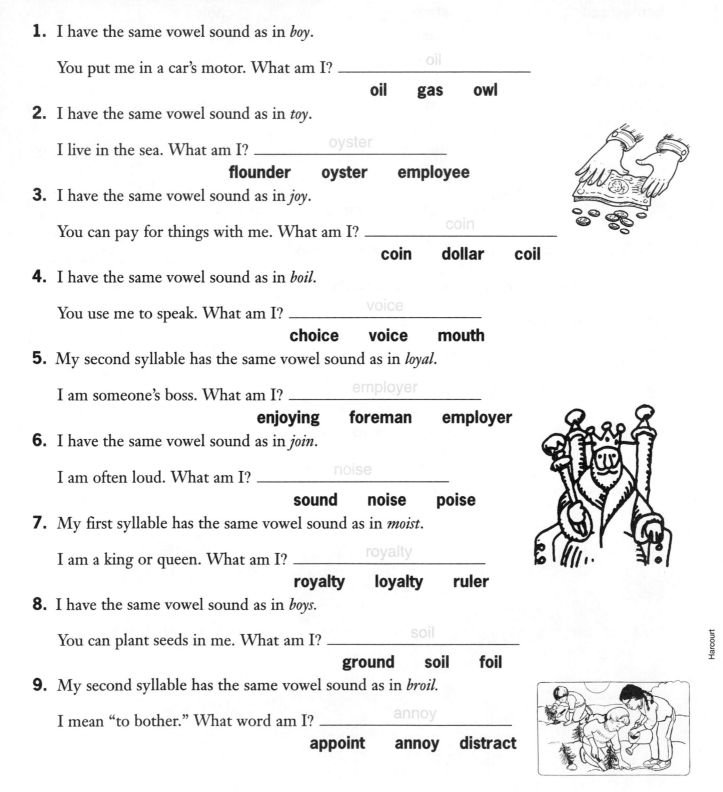

Harcourt

Peppermint-Peanut-Butter Fudge

Complete the sequence chart for "Peppermint-Peanut-Butter Fudge." Write a sentence in each box. The first one has been done for you.

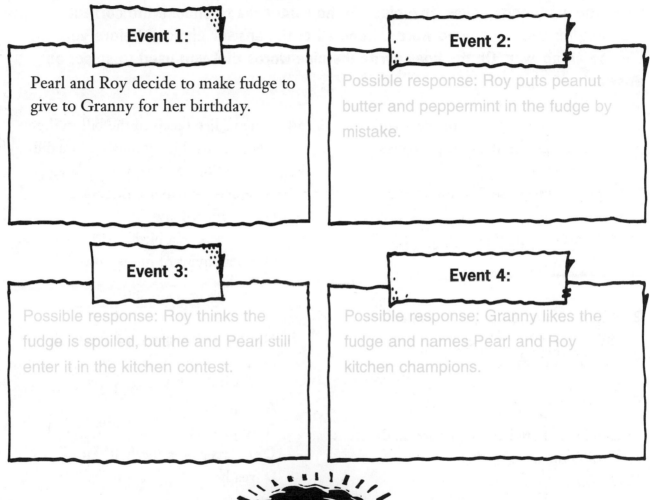

Event 1:

Pearl and Roy decide to make fudge to give to Granny for her birthday.

Event 2:

Possible response: Roy puts peanut butter and peppermint in the fudge by mistake.

Event 3:

Possible response: Roy thinks the fudge is spoiled, but he and Pearl still enter it in the kitchen contest.

Event 4:

Possible response: Granny likes the fudge and names Pearl and Roy kitchen champions.

Now use the information from the boxes to write a one-sentence summary of the selection.

Possible response: Pearl and Roy accidentally make peppermint-peanut-butter

fudge for Granny's birthday gift, and even though they think the fudge is no good,

Granny loves it.

Harcourt

Word Relationships

Multiple-meaning words are words that have more than one meaning. Use sentence and paragraph clues to decide the correct meaning of the word. Sometimes you can figure out the correct meaning by deciding the part of speech of the word.

Read the sentences below. Use clues in the sentences to choose the correct meaning for the underlined words. Read all of the answer choices before you choose an answer. On the lines, write the clue words that you used to select an answer.

1. Jessica is a <u>key</u> member of the team. She offers useful ideas for problems.
   A a low island
   B metal object used for unlocking
   C important
   D a part on a piano or typewriter

   team; useful ideas

2. My friend and I will <u>part</u> company after dinner. I won't see him until he returns from vacation.
   A separate
   B actor's role in a play
   C a line where hair is combed in different directions
   D piece

   returns from vacation

3. We were all surprised by how far he could <u>cast</u> the ball. It landed halfway across the field.
   A a heavy bandage
   B throw
   C select actors for a play
   D a shade

   ball; landed

4. When Alice received the <u>bill</u> in the mail, she paid it right away. She did not want her payment to be late.
   A a piece of paper money
   B a proposed law
   C the beak of a bird
   D a statement of money owed

   mail; payment

5. Our large dog sleeps by the front door every night. It has been trained to <u>guard</u> the house from any intruders.
   A a shield
   B to protect
   C a player on a football team
   D ready

   house; intruders

Harcourt

Fluency Builder

congested	king	audiences
patron	plays	law
dismantle	many	applause
adornment	company	flaws
critical	they	faults
shareholder	family	haughty
lavish	taught	

1. During the 1600s, / audiences were critical / of all dramas.

2. Molière was one / of four shareholders / in an acting company.

3. Molière's family / sent him to a college / to be taught law, / but he wanted to act.

4. They dismantled / their rolling stage in Paris / and performed / at congested theaters.

5. The king of France / became Molière's patron.

6. Molière based his plays / on the flaws and faults / of real people.

7. The king cherished Molière / as an adornment / to his court.

8. Many of Molière's plays / poked fun / at the haughty way / some rich people behaved.

9. Today / audiences still lavish / praise and applause / on Molière's plays.

A Man of the Theater

Read the story. Then circle the letter of the answer that makes each sentence below tell about the story.

"Let's hurry up and finish lunch. Our show is starting," said Saul. Saul and Dawn wanted to watch the new nature show on TV. It had been launched only two weeks ago. It was a big success.

The first part of today's show was about wild birds. "Is that a hawk?" asked Dawn.

"Yes," Saul said. "It saw a mouse and caught it with its claws. Hawks have to work hard for their lunch."

The second part featured trout. "I didn't know some trout live in the sea," Saul said.

"The narrator said they have to travel to fresh water to spawn," Dawn explained. "It's a long haul upstream to lay their eggs."

The last part was about deer. Saul said, "That fawn is eating plants near a lawn. Now it's yawning. I guess deer feel sleepy after lunch, too. This show has taught me all sorts of things about animals!"

1 What is today's nature show about?
  A how to make lunch
  B birds, trout, and deer
  C a mouse that catches a hawk
  D birds and insects

2 What did the hawk do?
  F It saw a rabbit.
  G It caught some lunch.
  H It landed on the lawn.
  J It crawled up a tree.

3 Why do trout swim upstream?
  A to launch a rocket
  B to haul a bale of straw
  C to cause a stir
  D to spawn

4 Where was the fawn?
  F on a seesaw
  G near someone's lawn
  H in a vault
  J in Saul's kitchen

5 What did the fawn do?
  A run across the lawn
  B draw a picture
  C yawn after eating
  D eat a prawn

6 What has the show done?
  F It has taught Saul about autumn.
  G It has shown astronauts.
  H It has told stories about authors.
  J It has taught Saul about animals.

Harcourt

Name_____

A Man of the Theater

Complete the sequence chart about "A Man of the Theater." Write a sentence in each box.

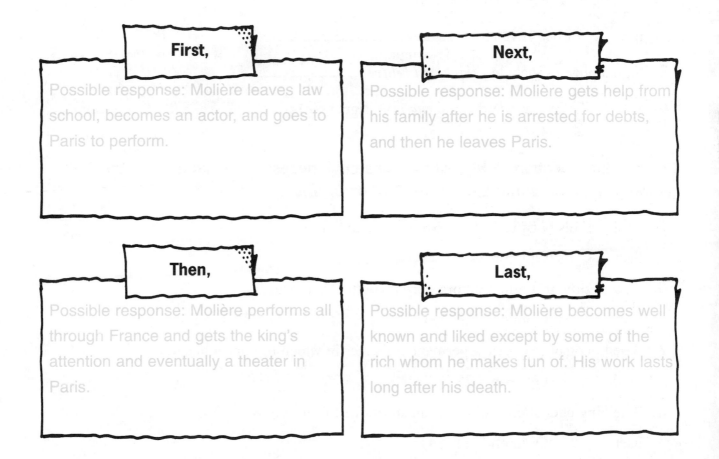

First,
Possible response: Molière leaves law school, becomes an actor, and goes to Paris to perform.

Next,
Possible response: Molière gets help from his family after he is arrested for debts, and then he leaves Paris.

Then,
Possible response: Molière performs all through France and gets the king's attention and eventually a theater in Paris.

Last,
Possible response: Molière becomes well known and liked except by some of the rich whom he makes fun of. His work lasts long after his death.

Now use the information from the boxes to write a one-sentence summary of the entire selection.

Possible response: Molière becomes a great playwright after a rocky start and despite criticism from the people he makes fun of.

Fact and Opinion

Read the sentences or phrases. In the blanks, write *fact* or *opinion*.

1. information that can be proven _____ fact _____

2. a thought or feeling about something

   that cannot be proven _____ opinion _____

3. Signal phrases include *I think* or *I believe*. _____ opinion _____

4. Words like *best, wonderful,* and *enjoyable,* signal a(n) _____ opinion _____

Refer to the selection "A Man of the Theater" if necessary. Read each of the following sentences and then circle *Fact* or *Opinion*.

5. Molière was born in 1622 into a well-to-do family.

   (Fact)   Opinion

6. At that time in France, actors were no better than beggars.

   Fact   (Opinion)

7. The king gave Molière a permanent theater in which to put on his plays.

   (Fact)   Opinion

8. The king cherished Molière as an adornment to his court.

   Fact   (Opinion)

9. In 1680, the main theater in France was named "The House of Molière."

   (Fact)   Opinion

10. Since then, theaters everywhere have been congested with huge crowds when Molière's plays are performed.

    Fact   (Opinion)

Harcourt

Fluency Builder

illustrating	pictures	books
series	full	good
encouraged	box	wooden
pastels	teacher	could
charcoal	draw	would
	world	took
	very	
	when	
	began	

1. Istvan Banyai began drawing / when he was very young. / A good teacher / encouraged him to draw.

2. In his grandmother's house / there were wooden boxes / full of old photos.

3. He experimented / with charcoal and pastels, / but he always begins / in pencil.

4. When he draws, / he makes a series / of pictures.

5. Illustrating / is his job. / Pictures for onc book / took Istvan Banyai / 120 hours to complete.

6. The light / inside the lantern / would flash onto the walls.

7. Using a pencil, / he could enter / an imaginary world.

8. Sometimes / he starts drawings / for a new book / by making dots.

My Imaginary World

**Read the story. Circle the words that have the vowel sound you hear in *took*
and *would*.**

Snook Stops a Crook!

Jenny owns a bookstore. Her cat, Snook, comes with her each day to her job. Snook likes to curl up in a peaceful nook in the back corner. Shoppers at the store will stop to look at the sleeping cat. "Would it be okay to pet him?" they ask Jenny. "Yes!" says Jenny with a smile. "He enjoys that!"

One day Snook helped catch a crook. A man was looking at the cookbooks while Jenny spoke with a customer. The man slid a book under his woolen coat. He would have left without paying for it, but he bumped into the sleeping cat with his foot by mistake. Snook sprang up surprised and took off running. The crook couldn't stop himself from tripping. He fell. The stolen book slipped out. It landed on the wooden steps.

After the police took the crook away, Jenny hugged Snook. "What a good cat you are!" she said. "You should get a prize!"

Now write the circled word that best completes each sentence.

1. Jenny's cat, _____ *Snook* _____, comes to work with her each day.

2. Snook likes to curl up in a quiet _____ *nook* _____ and sleep.

3. The cat once helped catch a _____ *crook* _____.

4. The man was looking at _____ *cookbooks* _____ in the store.

5. When Jenny wasn't looking, he put a book under his _____ *woolen* _____ coat.

6. He _____ *would* _____ have left without paying for it, but he tripped over the cat!

7. The police _____ *took* _____ the man away.

8. Jenny said her cat _____ *should* _____ get a prize!

Harcourt

Name _____

My Imaginary World

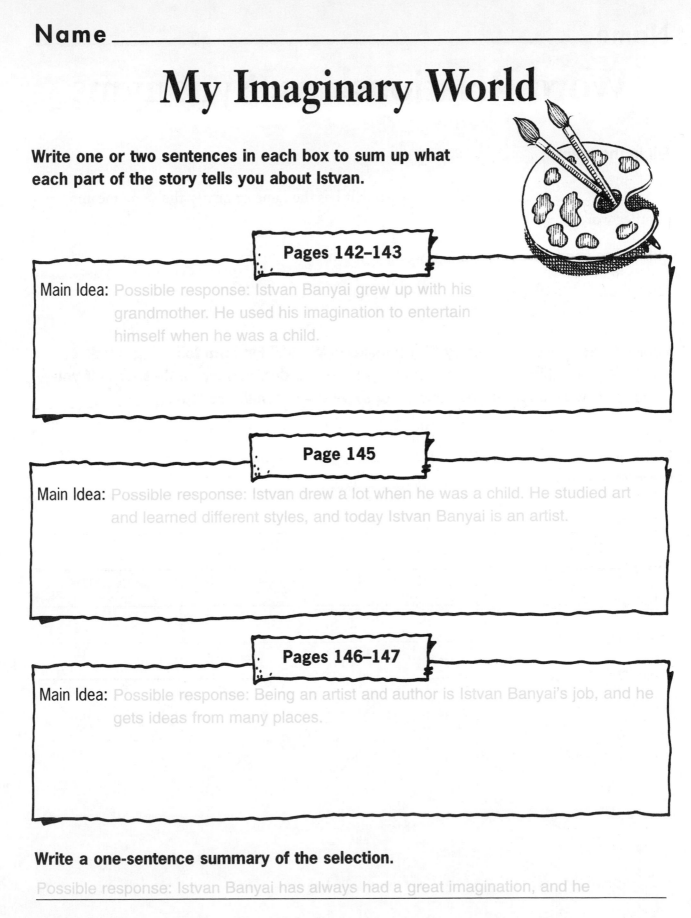

Write one or two sentences in each box to sum up what each part of the story tells you about Istvan.

Pages 142–143

Main Idea: Possible response: Istvan Banyai grew up with his grandmother. He used his imagination to entertain himself when he was a child.

Page 145

Main Idea: Possible response: Istvan drew a lot when he was a child. He studied art and learned different styles, and today Istvan Banyai is an artist.

Pages 146–147

Main Idea: Possible response: Being an artist and author is Istvan Banyai's job, and he gets ideas from many places.

Write a one-sentence summary of the selection.

Possible response: Istvan Banyai has always had a great imagination, and he

has used it to become an artist and author.

Word Relationships: Synonyms

Fill in the blanks.

A _____ synonym _____ is a word that has the same or nearly the same meaning as another word.

When you know the synonym of a word, you can figure out its

_____ meaning _____.

Look at page 145 in the story "My Imaginary World." Find the following words on page 145 and think of a synonym for each. Use a dictionary or a thesaurus if you need to. Check whether your choice of synonym will make sense.

Possible responses are given.

drawing _____ sketching _____

good _____ skillful, able _____

scary _____ frightening _____

funny _____ humorous _____

different _____ special, distinct _____

developed _____ created, made _____

complete _____ finish _____

Harcourt

Fluency Builder

pawnshop	sang	stoop
produce	near	music
errands	dance	new
numerous	star	afternoons
international	front	fool
gravelly	out	boost
	all	school

1. Ella lived / near a pawnshop / and a produce market / in New York City.

2. She sang / with her friends / on her front stoop / in the afternoons after school.

3. She could imitate the styles / of singers from the radio. / Some of their voices were smooth, / and some were gravelly.

4. When Ella was out running errands / with her friends, / they dared her / to enter a dance contest.

5. Her feet would not move, / so she had to do something / or look like a fool. / She sang.

6. Ella entered numerous contests / and won them all.

7. Ella Fitzgerald gave / her career a boost / by developing a new style / of singing called "scat." / She became / an international star.

With Love from Ella

Read the sentences and do what they tell you.

1. There is a ball in the pool. Draw the ball.
2. Give Andrew a hula hoop to play with.
3. Sue is holding a tool. Draw her tool.
4. Ruth has a bowl of stew. Draw her bowl.
5. Give Ruth a spoon, too.
6. Ruth's stool is missing. Draw a stool for her to sit on.
7. Sue has a cup of juice. Draw the cup.
8. Who threw a boot into the pool? Draw a boot in the water.
9. Andrew's swimsuit has stripes on it. Draw the stripes.
10. There are a few flowers blooming in the vase. Draw them there.
11. Andrew blew a big bubble with his gum. Draw the bubble.
12. A bird flew onto the roof. Put a bird there.
13. Draw a broom by the door.
14. The wind blew over a potted plant. Draw the plant coming out of the pot.
15. The plant's leaves are strewn around the pool. Draw a few leaves.

Now circle the words that have the long *oo* vowel sound.

Harcourt

With Love from Ella

Complete the sequence chart about "With Love from Ella." Write a sentence in each box. The first box has been done for you.

Event 1

Sixteen-year-old Ella Fitzgerald wins first prize for her singing in a contest.

Event 2

Possible response: Bandleader Chick Webb hires Ella to sing in his jazz band, and she becomes an international star.

Event 3

Possible response: Years later, Ella goes solo and develops a new style of music called "scat" singing.

Event 4

Possible response: Before she died in 1996, Ella won many honors and became a member of the National Women's Hall of Fame.

Now use the information from the boxes to write a one-sentence summary of the selection.

Possible response: Ella Fitzgerald followed her dream to become one of the world's

greatest singers of all time.

Fact and Opinion

A **fact** is something that can be proved. An **opinion** is a belief not necessarily based on fact.

Read the following sentences from the story "With Love from Ella." Decide whether each one is a fact or an opinion. On the blank next to each sentence, write F if the sentence is a fact, or O if it is an opinion.

Chick was also a composer and he wrote numerous songs. _____F_____

In 1938 I recorded one of them. _____F_____

It was called "A-Tisket, A-Tasket." _____F_____

It sold a million copies in only a couple of weeks and is still

one of my best-known songs. _____F_____

When Chick died, I felt so blue. _____F_____

I became the leader of our band and we played our music everywhere.

_____F_____

The public loved us, as jazz was very popular. _____O_____

After three years, however, I paused to consider my career. _____F_____

It was time for me to leave the band and go solo. _____O_____

Harcourt

Fluency Builder

migrant	**won**	**wrote**
timid	**full**	**wrapped**
flexibility	**days**	**wrong**
devote	**began**	**wriggled**
scholarship	**dance**	
thrived	**star**	
apprentice	**filled**	
	American	

1. The López family / migrated to Florida / from Cuba / when Lourdes was one year old.

2. While the clerk wrapped her shoes, / Lourdes wriggled her toes / into ballet shoes.

3. Lourdes devoted six days a week / to practicing ballet.

4. Lourdes won a full scholarship / to the School of American Ballet.

5. When she was 15, / Lourdes began her career / as an apprentice / with the New York City Ballet.

6. Lourdes was timid / when she first became a full member / of the New York City Ballet.

7. Lourdes didn't believe / she'd ever be a star, / but she was wrong.

8. Her life was filled / with hard work, / but she thrived on it.

9. Critics wrote / about Lourdes's flexibility / as a dancer.

Lourdes López: Ballet Star

Circle and write the word that best completes each sentence.

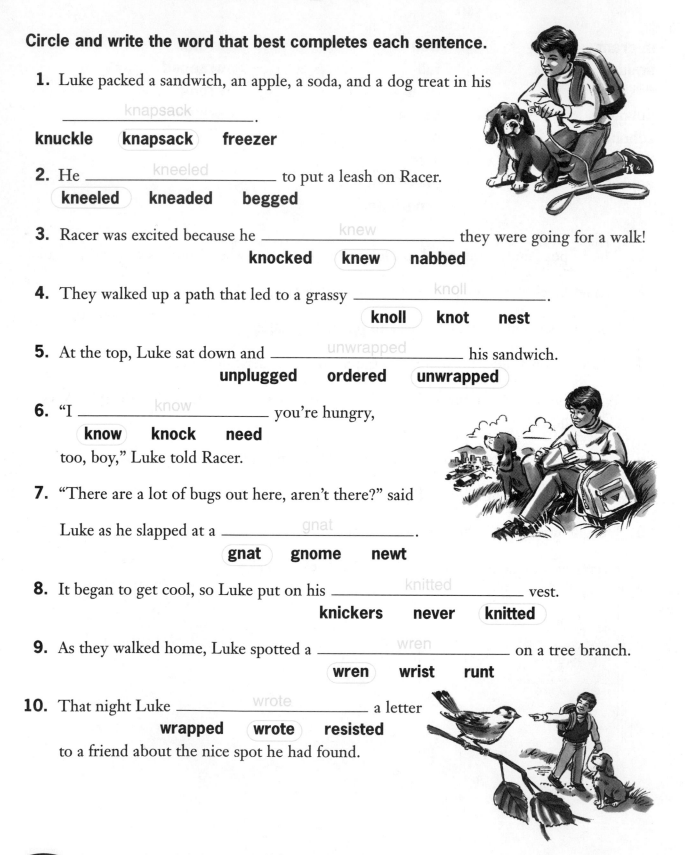

1. Luke packed a sandwich, an apple, a soda, and a dog treat in his

   _____knapsack_____.

   knuckle   (knapsack)   freezer

2. He _____kneeled_____ to put a leash on Racer.

   (kneeled)   kneaded   begged

3. Racer was excited because he _____knew_____ they were going for a walk!

   knocked   (knew)   nabbed

4. They walked up a path that led to a grassy _____knoll_____.

   (knoll)   knot   nest

5. At the top, Luke sat down and _____unwrapped_____ his sandwich.

   unplugged   ordered   (unwrapped)

6. "I _____know_____ you're hungry,

   (know)   knock   need

   too, boy," Luke told Racer.

7. "There are a lot of bugs out here, aren't there?" said

   Luke as he slapped at a _____gnat_____.

   (gnat)   gnome   newt

8. It began to get cool, so Luke put on his _____knitted_____ vest.

   knickers   never   (knitted)

9. As they walked home, Luke spotted a _____wren_____ on a tree branch.

   (wren)   wrist   runt

10. That night Luke _____wrote_____ a letter

    wrapped   (wrote)   resisted

    to a friend about the nice spot he had found.

Name_____

Lourdes López: Ballet Star

Complete the sequence chart about "Lourdes López: Ballet Star."
Write a sentence in each box. The first one has been done for you.

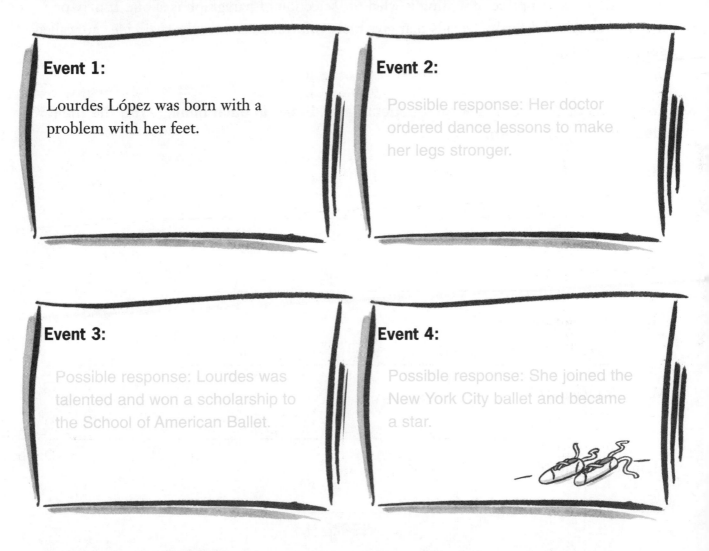

Event 1:

Lourdes López was born with a problem with her feet.

Event 2:

Possible response: Her doctor ordered dance lessons to make her legs stronger.

Event 3:

Possible response: Lourdes was talented and won a scholarship to the School of American Ballet.

Event 4:

Possible response: She joined the New York City ballet and became a star.

Now use the information from the boxes to write a one-sentence summary of the selection.

Possible response: Lourdes López overcame foot problems to become a ballet star.

Harcourt

Text Structure: Main Idea and Details

The **main idea** of a piece of writing is what the selection or paragraph is about. It may or may not be stated directly. Details that give more information about the main idea are called **supporting details**.

Look back at the story "Lourdes López: Ballet Star." In each blank, write the main idea for the page given.

Main Idea, page 158

As a young girl, Lourdes was attracted to ballet. _____

Main Idea, page 159

Lourdes had to take ballet to make her feet stronger and grew to love it. _____

Main Idea, page 160

Lourdes moved to New York at 14 to study ballet seriously. _____

Main Idea, page 163

Lourdes became an apprentice and ultimately a star ballerina. _____

Main Idea, page 164

Lourdes has stayed involved with dance no matter what. _____

What is the main idea for the whole selection?

Lourdes fell in love with ballet and made it to the top with much hard work. ___

Harcourt

Fluency Builder

campaign	standing	laughed
residence	maybe	photo
obnoxious	chair	phrases
endorse	eye	emphasis
graffiti	I'll	geography
	front	Murphy
	some	
	ask	
	said	

1. During the campaign, / Al wore a T-shirt / with his photo on it.

2. A portrait of Lincoln / standing in front /of one of his residences / caught Murphy's eye.

3. Murphy thought / Al was acting obnoxious.

4. Murphy and several / other students erased / some graffiti / from the wall.

5. Al laughed / at Murphy's emphasis / on a campaign platform. / "Maybe I'll stand / on a chair / when I give my speech," / he said.

6. Al asked the crossing guard / to endorse his campaign.

7. During geography, / Murphy heard whispered phrases / that included his name.

8. Al asked / the other students / to vote for the best candidate.

Harcourt

Name _____

Certain Steps

Read the story. Circle all the words with the /f/ sound spelled *gh* or *ph*.

Phyllis and her father went to the zoo in Philadelphia. Phyllis is five years old. This was her first trip to the zoo. First they went to see the African elephants. The baby elephant trumpeted emphatically and made Phyllis laugh. Phyllis asked her father to take photos of it. She hoped to show the photographs to her brother Murphy. Then they went to see the giraffes. Phyllis thought they looked tall enough to reach the clouds! She asked her father to take photos of the giraffes, too. Then Phyllis asked the zookeeper to autograph the photo. Her emphasis on getting the autograph surprised her father.

"Why did you ask the zookeeper to sign the photo?" her father asked.

"That way Murphy will know the photos aren't phony," she said. Her response made her father laugh.

Circle and write the word that best completes each sentence.

1. Phyllis and her father visited the zoo in ___Philadelphia___.

   Pennsylvania   Flowerville   Philadelphia

2. Their first stop was to see the ___elephants___.

   graphs   elephants   panthers

3. Her father took lots of ___photographs___ of the baby elephant.

   photographs   alphabets   autographs

4. Phyllis wanted to show them to ___Murphy___.

   Ralph   Murphy   Philip

5. She asked the zookeeper for an ___autograph___.

   alphabet   elephant   autograph

6. Phyllis made her father ___laugh___.

   talk   laugh   frown

Harcourt

Certain Steps

Write a sentence or sentences in each box below to summarize the selection. Be sure to write the events in correct order.

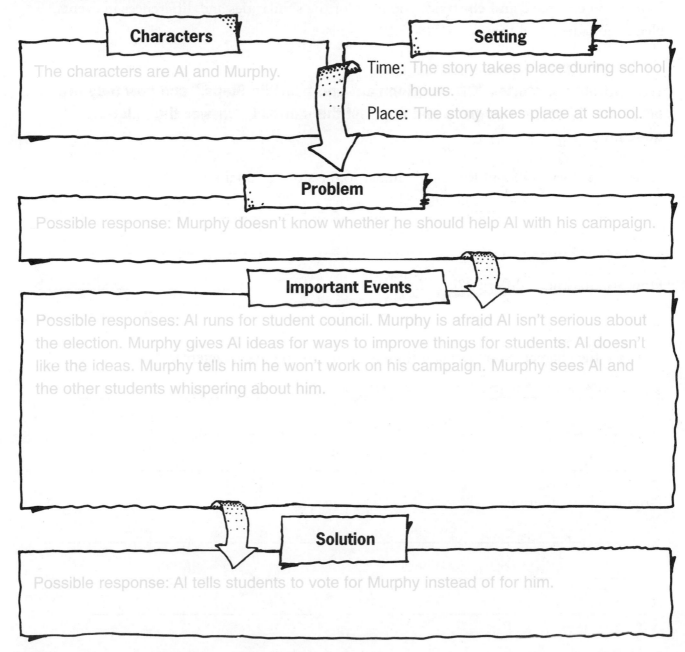

Characters

The characters are Al and Murphy.

Setting

Time: The story takes place during school hours.

Place: The story takes place at school.

Problem

Possible response: Murphy doesn't know whether he should help Al with his campaign.

Important Events

Possible responses: Al runs for student council. Murphy is afraid Al isn't serious about the election. Murphy gives Al ideas for ways to improve things for students. Al doesn't like the ideas. Murphy tells him he won't work on his campaign. Murphy sees Al and the other students whispering about him.

Solution

Possible response: Al tells students to vote for Murphy instead of for him.

Now write a one-sentence summary of the story.

Possible response: Murphy tells Al he won't help him run for student council, but

instead of becoming angry with Murphy, Al tells everyone to vote for Murphy.

Text Structure: Compare and Contrast

When you **compare and contrast**, you look for the similarities and differences in events, characters, ideas, and things.

Think about the stories "Off and Running" and "Certain Steps," and how they are alike and different. Compare and contrast the stories to answer the following questions.

How is the story "Off and Running" similar to the story "Certain Steps"?

Both are stories about school elections.

_____

How are the stories different? Murphy is a surprise candidate while Miata has been

working hard on her campaign.

How are the characters in "Off and Running" similar to the characters in "Certain Steps"?

Both Miata and Murphy are serious about wanting to improve their school.

Neither Al nor Ruby are serious about their campaigns.

_____

How are they different? Murphy doesn't plan to run. Miata does and uses her

family and other outside resources to help her win. Al gives his support to Murphy,

while Rudy gives Miata a hard time by making an annoying phone call.

_____

Harcourt

Fluency Builder

polio	idea	threatened
decipher	some	instead
astonishment	who	spread
immobility	once	threat
dismay	many	dead
despised	believe	
	help	
	that	
	doctor	

1. At one time / some people who contracted polio / had to live a life of immobility / in an iron lung.

2. The spread of flu / once threatened people's lives.

3. Jonas Salk chose / to become a doctor / instead of a lawyer.

4. Dr. Salk's research required / a great deal of time / to decipher enormous amounts of data.

5. Dr. Salk hit many dead ends / before he finally discovered / a vaccine for polio.

6. Dr. Salk was astonished and dismayed / by his fame.

7. Dr. Salk despised the idea / of making money / from a vaccine needed to save lives.

8. Jonas Salk believed / that it is important for us / to do something / that helps humanity / as well as ourselves.

Quest for a Healthy World

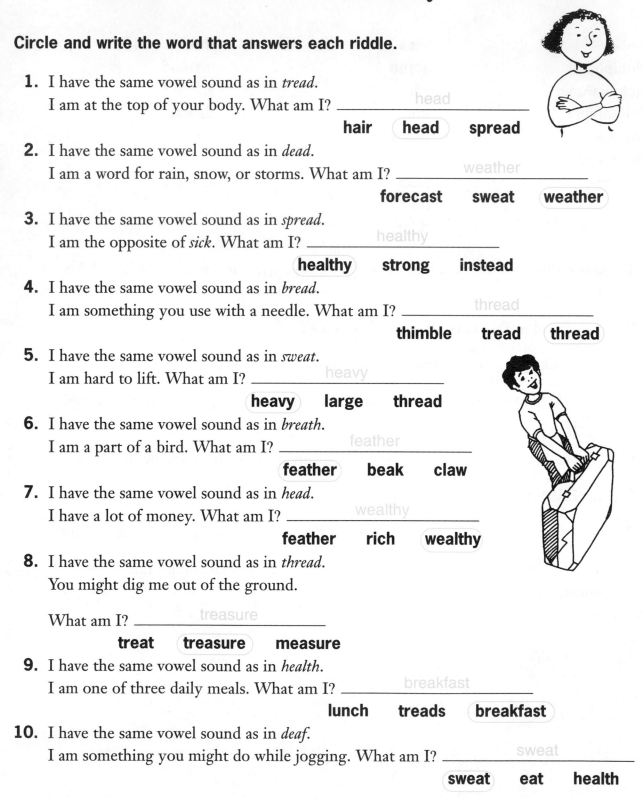

Circle and write the word that answers each riddle.

1. I have the same vowel sound as in *tread.*
   I am at the top of your body. What am I? _____ head

   hair   (head)   spread

2. I have the same vowel sound as in *dead.*
   I am a word for rain, snow, or storms. What am I? _____ weather

   forecast   sweat   (weather)

3. I have the same vowel sound as in *spread.*
   I am the opposite of *sick.* What am I? _____ healthy

   (healthy)   strong   instead

4. I have the same vowel sound as in *bread.*
   I am something you use with a needle. What am I? _____ thread

   thimble   tread   (thread)

5. I have the same vowel sound as in *sweat.*
   I am hard to lift. What am I? _____ heavy

   (heavy)   large   thread

6. I have the same vowel sound as in *breath.*
   I am a part of a bird. What am I? _____ feather

   (feather)   beak   claw

7. I have the same vowel sound as in *head.*
   I have a lot of money. What am I? _____ wealthy

   feather   rich   (wealthy)

8. I have the same vowel sound as in *thread.*
   You might dig me out of the ground.

   What am I? _____ treasure

   treat   (treasure)   measure

9. I have the same vowel sound as in *health.*
   I am one of three daily meals. What am I? _____ breakfast

   lunch   treads   (breakfast)

10. I have the same vowel sound as in *deaf.*
    I am something you might do while jogging. What am I? _____ sweat

    (sweat)   eat   health

Harcourt

Name _____

Quest for a Healthy World

Write one sentence in each box below to tell about Jonas Salk.

Pages 174–175

Main Idea: Possible response: Jonas Salk became a medical scientist.

Page 176

Main Idea: Possible response: He showed that it was possible to make a vaccine against the flu virus.

Pages 177–178

Main Idea: Possible response: He developed a polio vaccine that made him famous, but he didn't want to make money on it.

Pages 179–180

Main Idea: Possible response: He believed that his mother was his best teacher and that people should help others as well as themselves.

Write a one-sentence summary statement about the selection.

Possible response: Dr. Jonas Salk helped many people by developing flu and

polio vaccines.

Harcourt

Author's Purpose and Perspective

An **author's purpose** is the reason he or she writes the selection. The author's purpose can be to entertain, to inform, or to persuade. An **author's perspective** includes his or her opinions, attitudes, and feelings about the topic.

Look back at the story "Quest for a Healthy World." What do you think is the author's purpose for writing this selection?

to inform

Here is a passage from the selection. Reread it and answer the question that follows.

Jonas Salk never applied for a patent on his polio vaccine. It would have made him rich, but he believed that such things must belong to humanity. There was a big hubbub among his peers, who said he could use the money for his research. It just seemed wrong to Dr. Salk. He despised the idea of making money from a vaccine needed to save lives. He would find other ways to raise money for his research.

What do you think are some of the author's opinions and ideas about Jonas Salk and medicine?

Possible response: Doctors should be more concerned about saving lives.

Doctors should not be concerned with making money. Dr. Salk was a very good man.

Look at the rest of the selection in your book. Write down two other attitudes or opinions you think the author has. What makes you think that?

Possible response: It's important to do good things to help other people. The author

focuses on Dr. Salk's unselfishness and makes it sound honorable.

Fluency Builder

insulated	noise	eight
muffle	cat	freight
partition	tried	veil
prowls	rope	weight
refinery	idea	break
grade	called	
submitted	around	
	would	

1. The loud noise / of the nearby refinery / did not wake Pete, nor did the early morning / freight train.

2. When Pete was asleep, / a mysterious veil / seemed to muffle all his senses.

3. "He wants to break his record," / Mark called out. / "He's been late / eight days in a row."

4. Pete was afraid / his grades would slip. / What could he do?

5. He insulated one wall / of his bedroom with blankets, / so his alarm would not / wake his grandma.

6. He tied a weight / to the end / of a rope. Pete tried to make / a cardboard partition / to fit around his bed.

7. Pete's cat / prowls the house / at night.

8. Pete submitted / his alarm / to the class invention fair.

9. "Now / that's what I call / an original idea!" / Mark called out.

Pete's Great Invention

**Read the story. Then read each question. Decide which is the best answer.
Circle the letter or statement for that answer.**

Diana's neighbor Seth owns eight Great Danes. Great Danes are very large dogs. They can weigh up to 175 pounds! Seth's dogs can lick his face when they stand up on their hind legs.

Seth told Diana that together the dogs weighed more than a thousand pounds. After that Diana started calling the dogs the "heavyweights." Diana likes to tease Seth about his dogs. One day Seth told Diana that he feeds the dogs raw steak. Diana asked if the dogs' food had to be delivered by freight train.

At daybreak Seth takes his eight dogs for a walk. Diana likes to watch them from her window. She thinks the dogs' leashes look like reins. Once she told Seth that he should make fake antlers for his dogs. Then they could be his very own reindeer! "Seth driving a sleigh—how funny!" she said to herself. Seth didn't think it was such a great idea. It did make him laugh, however.

1 Who is Seth?
  A Diana's great-grandfather
  B a sleigh driver
  C a lightweight boxer
  D Diana's neighbor

2 What does Seth own?
  F eighteen Great Lakes
  G eight Great Danes
  H a freight train
  J eight reindeer

3 Why does Diana call the dogs the "heavyweights"?
  A They weigh eight tons.
  B They break sleighs.
  C Together, they weigh more than a thousand pounds.
  D They neigh like horses.

4 What does Seth feed the Great Danes?
  F chow mein
  G paperweights
  H reins
  J raw steak

5 Diana asked if the dogs' food is delivered by
  A a freight train.
  B a sleigh.
  C a neighbor.
  D a great supermarket.

6 When do the dogs go for a walk?
  F after a great meal
  G while unveiling a statue
  H at daybreak
  J every eight days

Harcourt

Pete's Great Invention

Complete the sequence chart about "Pete's Great Invention." Write a sentence in each box. The first one is done for you.

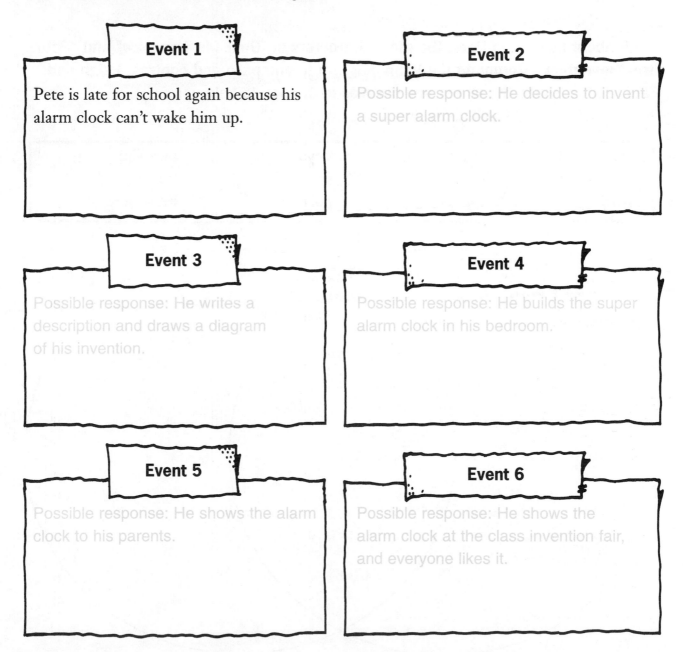

Event 1

Pete is late for school again because his alarm clock can't wake him up.

Event 2

Possible response: He decides to invent a super alarm clock.

Event 3

Possible response: He writes a description and draws a diagram of his invention.

Event 4

Possible response: He builds the super alarm clock in his bedroom.

Event 5

Possible response: He shows the alarm clock to his parents.

Event 6

Possible response: He shows the alarm clock at the class invention fair, and everyone likes it.

Write a one-sentence summary statement about the selection.

Possible response: Pete invents a super alarm clock so that he won't be late for school anymore.

Compare and Contrast

When you **compare and contrast**, you find similarities and differences. You can compare and contrast characters, places, events, objects, and ideas.

Think about Leigh and Pete, the main characters in "Dear Mr. Henshaw" and "Pete's Great Invention." Complete the Venn diagram to compare and contrast Leigh and Pete. You may use the words and phrases in the box to help you.

Possible responses are given.

problem	noisy	boys	deadline
grandmother	writer	school	tardy
award	home	parents	invention

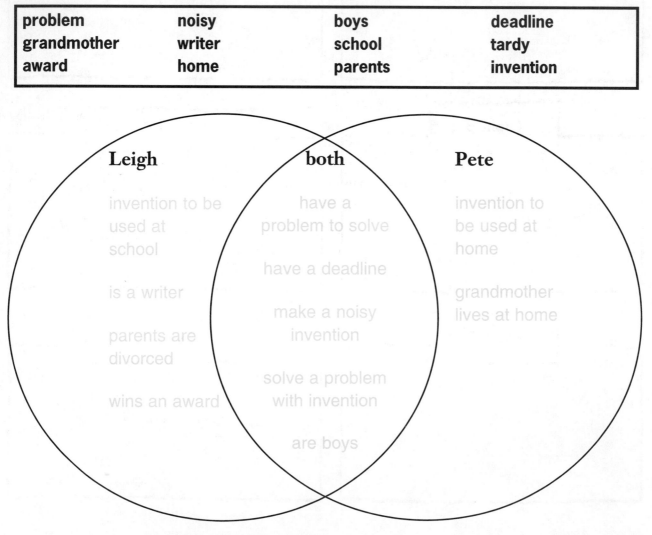

Leigh

invention to be used at school

is a writer

parents are divorced

wins an award

both

have a problem to solve

have a deadline

make a noisy invention

solve a problem with invention

are boys

Pete

invention to be used at home

grandmother lives at home

Harcourt

Fluency Builder

beaming	guessed	dumb
reputation	first	solemn
sidetrack	board	numb
absorbed	would	column
aisle	when	comb
oath	anything	honor
word	your	
	their	

1. The winners got points / added to their column / on the board.

2. Jenna's team could not let anything / sidetrack them. / Their reputation / and their honor / were at stake.

3. They took a solemn oath / to win the pizza.

4. First, / they would not / ask dumb questions.

5. Colin's team asked, / "Can you comb your hair / with it?"

6. Jenna was so absorbed / in listening to the questions, / that she dropped her kazoo / in the aisle.

7. Jenna was beaming / when she guessed / the correct answer.

8. The other teams / sat numb / with surprise.

One of a Kind

Read the sentences and do what they tell you.

1. Marty is sitting on a tree limb. Draw the limb he is sitting on.
2. Noni will climb the tree next. Add a rope to help her climb.
3. Marty is eating a cookie. Draw some crumbs falling from the cookie.
4. A lamb followed Noni and Marty to the tree. Give the lamb a name tag and a name.
5. Noni asks Marty if he reads her column in the class paper. Draw a speech balloon next to Noni, and write in her question.
6. Marty is honest. He says, "No." Draw a speech balloon next to Marty, and write "No" in it.
7. There is a beehive in the tree! Draw bees next to the honeycomb.
8. Noni sees the bees and whistles to Marty. Draw a whistle for her to use.
9. Marty is not listening. Put an X over his ear to show that he does not hear Noni.
10. A bee stings Marty's thumb. Draw the bee.
11. Noni feels bad that Marty got stung. She gives the thumbs-down signal. Draw it.
12. Marty does not cry often, but he starts to cry now. Draw tears on his face.

Now circle the words that have a silent _b_, _t_, _n_, or _h_.

One of a Kind

Write sentences in the boxes below to summarize the selection. Be sure to write the events in the correct order.

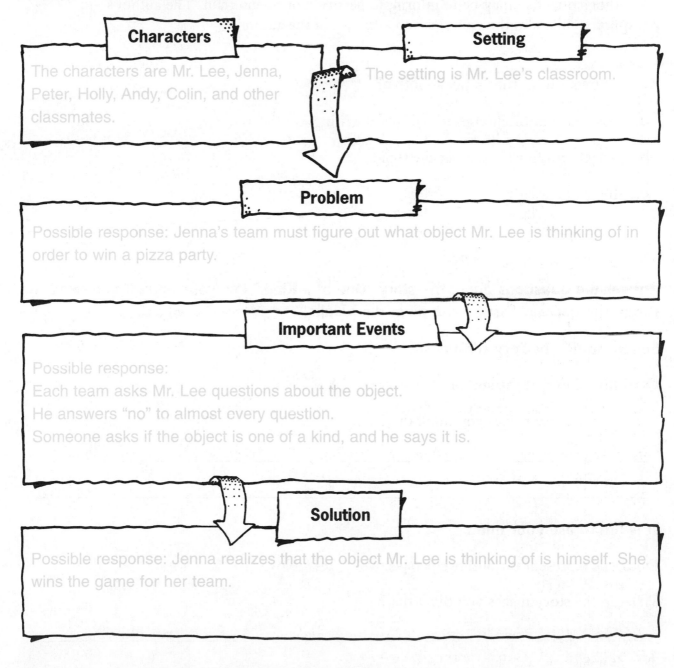

Characters

The characters are Mr. Lee, Jenna, Peter, Holly, Andy, Colin, and other classmates.

Setting

The setting is Mr. Lee's classroom.

Problem

Possible response: Jenna's team must figure out what object Mr. Lee is thinking of in order to win a pizza party.

Important Events

Possible response:
Each team asks Mr. Lee questions about the object.
He answers "no" to almost every question.
Someone asks if the object is one of a kind, and he says it is.

Solution

Possible response: Jenna realizes that the object Mr. Lee is thinking of is himself. She wins the game for her team.

Now write a one-sentence summary of the story.

Possible response: Jenna wins a pizza party for her team by figuring out that

the one-of-a-kind object Mr. Lee is thinking of is himself.

Harcourt

Author's Purpose and Perspective

Read the paragraph. Then read the question and circle the correct answers.

An author's **purpose** may be to inform, to persuade or to entertain. The author's **perspective** includes the opinions and attitudes of the author.

What shows the author's perspective?

a. what the author chooses to put in the writing

b. how the author feels about the topic

c. the words used

d. all of the above

Answer the questions about the story "One of a Kind." Use your book if you need to. Circle the correct answer and fill in the blanks.

School should be very serious.

Does this represent the author's perspective?   Yes   (No)

What in the story makes you think that?

Possible response: The teacher plays a game with the students and laughs a lot.

_____

It is fun to use your mind.

Does this represent the author's perspective?   (Yes)   No

What in the story makes you think that?

Possible response: Jenna works hard to figure out the answer and has fun doing it.

_____

Harcourt

Fluency Builder

sorrowfully	many	thoroughly
loftily	when	thought
dispute	found	tough
adjusted	talked	although
nonchalantly	called	
	once	
	they	
	how	
	said	
	knew	
	there	

1. There was a dispute / among the leaders.

2. Many were thoroughly scornful / of the Detroit project.

3. When jet tubes werc invented, / people adjusted / to horizontal travel.

4. The diary writer found it tough / to get comfortable / in an automobile.

5. The manual talked loftily / about the wonders / of the convertible.

6. Solomon nonchalantly / broke into a shuffle / that he called dancing.

7. Although he once owned an automobile, / Solomon sorrowfully said / that it was not a convertible.

8. They thought / those people knew / how to have fun.

What a Time It Was!

Read the story, and circle all the words with _ough_.

Maya and Alden thought they saw something flash in a tree. "Look, it went through those branches," said Maya. "We ought to find out what it is." They could see the tiny object move through the leaves. Finally, the small blur got close enough to be identified.

Alden was thoroughly delighted. "It's a hummingbird!" he exclaimed. The bird was tiny, but it was as bright as a jewel.

The little bird zipped out of sight behind a branch. The children sought to find it among the leaves. "Tough luck," Maya said. "We lost sight of it."

"It must be rough to be so small in this gigantic world," said Alden. "I hope that little bird has enough to eat. Maybe we can help. We could put up the hummingbird feeder that my mom bought."

Maya and Alden brought the feeder with them on their next trip to the park.

Now write the word with _ough_ that best completes each sentence.

1. Maya said they _____ to find out what the flash was.

2. The hummingbird _____ delighted Alden.

3. The hummingbird flew _____ the branches.

4. Maya thought it was _____ luck when they lost sight of the bird.

5. Alden thought it must be _____ to be so small.

6. Alden said he hoped the bird had _____ food.

7. Alden's mom had _____ a hummingbird feeder.

8. The friends _____ the feeder with them next time.

Name_____

What a Time It Was!

Write one sentence in each box below describing what the diary writer discovered that day.

Monday

> The writer found there were cars.

Tuesday

> The cars were uncomfortable then because you had to sit upright.

Wednesday

> The cars were slow and small.

Thursday

> The cars didn't last very long.

Friday

> The cars had airbags because they were likely to have accidents on two-way roads.

Saturday

> There were convertibles and campers.

Sunday

> The music that could be played on the CD in the car was wonderful and made one want to move.

Use the information in the chart to write a one-sentence summary of the selection.

Possible response: An explorer from the future discovers our cars of today, which he
doesn't like, but finds our music quite wonderful.

Harcourt

Draw Conclusions

When we read, we can **draw conclusions**. We can draw conclusions from the words and actions of the characters, the information the author tells us directly, and what we know.

Read the following conclusions that could be drawn from reading the story "What a Time It Was!" What information in the story would lead one to each of the conclusions?

Conclusion: The diary writer didn't think much of the "old" automobiles.

Possible responses: cars were uncomfortable; cars were slow; cars got in accidents;

cars didn't last very long.

_____

Conclusion: The diary writer discovered there were some good things about the old days.

Possible responses: you could play music in cars; music was fun to listen to;

dancing to the music was fun.

_____

Conclusion: The diary writer had never seen a CD until Solomon played one.

Possible responses: The diary writer didn't know that CDs have music on them. He

describes CDs as if they are strange and unusual.

_____

Fluency Builder

rigging	world	disliked
furl	wanted	unhappy
huddled	would	discouraged
vast	sea	unsafe
beams	father	
lurked	across	
settlement	between	
	idea	
	because	

1. The voyage / of Christopher Columbus led / to the settlement / of the New World.

2. Manolo Sánchez wanted / to become a sailor. / His mother / disliked the idea.

3. Manolo was not discouraged / when the sailors / would tease him.

4. Manolo and his father / sailed with Columbus / across the vast blue sea.

5. One unhappy day / a terrible storm came up.

6. Water seepcd / between the beams / and the wind ripped through the rigging.

7. Danger lurked everywhere, / so the sailors / huddled below the deck.

8. The crew furled the sails / because it would be unsafe / to leave them open.

Name

A Safe Harbor

Circle and write the word that best completes each sentence.

1. Alvin's mother was ___displeased___ when she saw his room.
   displayed   disproved   (displeased)

2. "I've been too busy ___reassembling___ my bicycle to clean my room," Alvin said.   **repackaging   (reassembling)   reconsidering**

3. "No more work on your bike until you ___reorganize___ your belongings," his mother said.   **(reorganize)   reopen   replace**

4. "But that's ___unfair___!" Alvin cried. "I need to fix my bike so I can
   unfriendly   unwise   (unfair)
   ride with the bike club today!"

5. "Enough," said Alvin's mother. "When I ___reappear___ in one hour, your room had better be clean."   **(reappear)   reconsider   remake**

6. Alvin sat down on his bed and stared

   at the mess ___unhappily___.
   unavoidably   (unhappily)   uncontrollably

7. "You could start by ___restacking___
   (restacking)   releasing   redirecting
   your books on the shelves," said his sister Ella.

8. "Why are you being so helpful?" asked Alvin
   ___uncertainly___.

   unstoppably   unluckily   (uncertainly)

9. "I know how important it is to you to fix your bike so you can

   ___rejoin___ the bike club," Ella explained.
   (rejoin)   replay   rejoice

10. "Boy, do I owe you one!" Alvin exclaimed as they started to

    ___reorder___ his toys.
    remodel   redesign   (reorder)

Harcourt

A Safe Harbor

**Complete the sequence chart about "A Safe Harbor."
Write a sentence in each box. The first box has been
done for you.**

Event 1

Manolo's father is hired as a cook on
Christopher Columbus's ship, and Manolo
gets to go on the trip to help out.

Event 2

Manolo helps out in many different ways,
and he doesn't mind it when the sailors
tease him.

Event 3

One day a terrible storm comes up, and
the ship is in danger of sinking because
the sails are not lowered.

Event 4

Manolo is the only crew member brave
enough to climb up the rigging and lower
the sails, and he saves the ship.

**Now use the information from the boxes to write a one-sentence summary of
the selection.**

Possible response: When Manolo gets to sail on Christopher Columbus's ship, he

proves his bravery by saving the ship in a storm.

Harcourt

Connotation/Denotation

The **denotation** of a word is its dictionary definition. The **connotation** of a word refers to additional feelings and ideas that the word suggests. A word may have positive or negative connotations.

Read the paragraph below.

One day a terrible storm came up. Waves nearly <u>flooded</u> the deck, and the ship tipped left and right, <u>struggling</u> to stay upright. Water seeping between the beams made us fear that the ship would sink. Danger from the storm <u>lurked</u> everywhere, but I tried to be <u>hopeful</u>.

Use a dictionary to write the denotation for each word below. Think about how the words are used in the paragraph. For each word, decide if the connotation is positive or negative. Circle the correct answer.

Flooded

Denotation ___overflowed with water_____

Connotation: Positive or (Negative)

Struggling

Denotation ___trying hard_____

Connotation: Positive or (Negative)

Lurked

Denotation ___waited in hiding_____

Connotation: Positive or (Negative)

Hopeful

Denotation ___having a feeling that something good will happen_____

Connotation: (Positive) or Negative

Harcourt

Fluency Builder

guarantee	women	carefully
distinguished	stumps	assuredly
misleading	many	softly
indebted	their	thoughtful
interpreter	were	
suffrage	would	
anthem	says	
	could	
	group	
	right	

1. James and Lucretia Mott / were criticized for their views / on women's suffrage.

2. They could not guarantee / their distinguished guest's safety.

3. James says / that a thoughtful and just interpreter / would assuredly admit / his actions were right.

4. It would be misleading / to call the mystery guest / a celebrity.

5. Lucretia and Beth placed / bundles of food / on the tree stumps / by the woodshed.

6. Many escaped slaves were indebted / to the Underground Railroad.

7. The group joined hands / and softly sang the anthem, / "Free at Last."

8. Beth carefully / hid nearby.

The Mystery Guest

Circle and write the word that answers each riddle.

1. You can wash me. What am I? _____ washable _____

  (**washable**)   unwashable   watchful

2. I mean "full of color." What am I? _____ colorful _____

  uncolorful   coloring   (**colorful**)

3. You can easily get around me. What am I? _____ avoidable _____

  avoidance   unavoidable   (**avoidable**)

4. I mean "in a way that is honest." What am I? _____ honestly _____

  honesty   (**honestly**)   dishonestly

5. I mean "without thought." What am I? _____ thoughtless _____

  thoughtful   (**thoughtless**)   thoughtfully

6. I mean "very sad." What am I? _____ sorrowful _____

  unsorrowful   sorrily   (**sorrowful**)

7. You enjoy having me around. What am I? _____ enjoyable _____

  (**enjoyable**)   joyless   unenjoyable

8. I mean "in a sad way." What am I? _____ sadly _____

  sad   (**sadly**)   saddle

9. I mean "without end." What am I? _____ endless _____

  (**endless**)   ending   ended

10. I am filled with respect if I act this way. What am I? _____ respectful _____

  disrespectful   returned   (**respectful**)

Harcourt

The Mystery Guest

Complete the sequence chart about "The Mystery Guest." Write a sentence in each box. The first one is done for you.

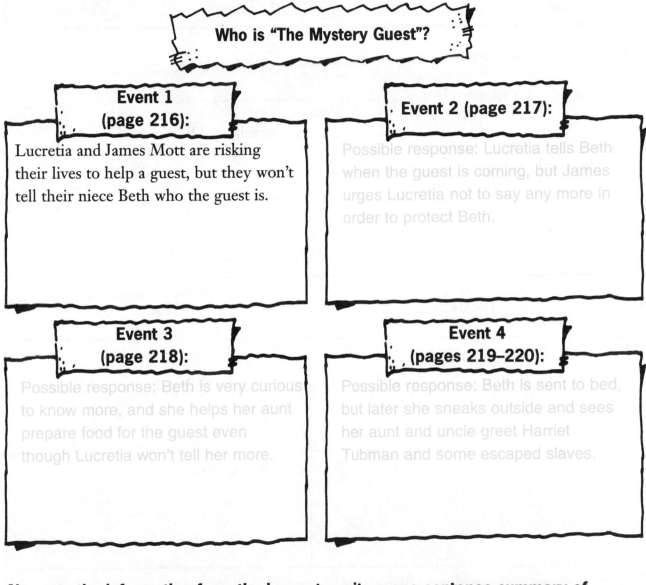

Who is "The Mystery Guest"?

Event 1 (page 216):

Lucretia and James Mott are risking their lives to help a guest, but they won't tell their niece Beth who the guest is.

Event 2 (page 217):

Possible response: Lucretia tells Beth when the guest is coming, but James urges Lucretia not to say any more in order to protect Beth.

Event 3 (page 218):

Possible response: Beth is very curious to know more, and she helps her aunt prepare food for the guest even though Lucretia won't tell her more.

Event 4 (pages 219–220):

Possible response: Beth is sent to bed, but later she sneaks outside and sees her aunt and uncle greet Harriet Tubman and some escaped slaves.

Now use the information from the boxes to write a one-sentence summary of the play.

Possible response: Aunt Lucretia and Uncle James won't tell Beth who their mystery guest will be, but Beth sneaks outside and learns that her aunt and uncle have risked their lives to help Harriet Tubman and some escaped slaves.

Harcourt

Name _____

Cause and Effect

Fill in the blanks with words from the box.

since	cause	therefore	effect

1. What happens because of some action or event is called a(n) _____ effect _____.

2. The reason it happens is the _____ cause _____.

3. The word _____ since _____ may be followed by a cause.

4. The word _____ therefore _____ may be followed by an effect.

Fill in the boxes.

Cause	Effect
Because Beth overhears her aunt and uncle talking about trouble,	Possible response: they tell her a guest is coming.
Possible response: Her aunt and uncle are worried and don't want her to know the identity of their mystery guest.	As a result, Beth is sent to bed.
Because Beth sneaks outdoors when she is supposed to be in bed,	Possible response: she gets to see that their guest is Harriet Tubman.

Harcourt

Name_____

Fluency Builder

edition
suspended
honors
contraption
repeal
treaty

worked
early
almost
many
first
kite
his
their
was
chair
write

nonexistent
impossible
impractical

1. In the early 1730s / novels were almost nonexistent / and nearly impossible to get.

2. Benjamin Franklin was the inventor / of many odd contraptions.

3. Franklin published the first edition / of *Poor Richard's Almanack* in 1733.

4. Ben Franklin suspended a key / from a kite / and proved / that lightning was electricity.

5. During his long life, / Franklin won many honors, / and worked on many / important matters.

6. Franklin got the British / to repeal some of their taxes / on the colonies.

7. After the colonies won their independence from England, / Benjamin Franklin helped write / the peace treaty.

8. Benjamin Franklin's inventions / included a rocking chair.

Harcourt

Name _____

Who Was Poor Richard?

Read the story. Circle each word that has one of these prefixes: *im-*, *non-*, or *pre-*.

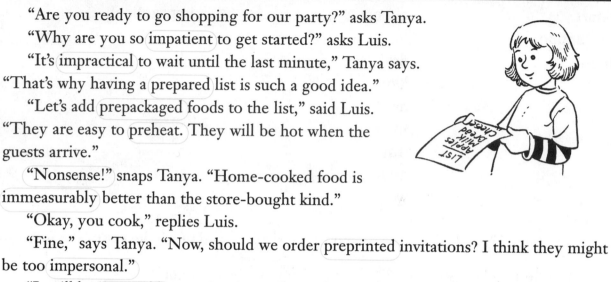

"Are you ready to go shopping for our party?" asks Tanya.

"Why are you so impatient to get started?" asks Luis.

"It's impractical to wait until the last minute," Tanya says. "That's why having a prepared list is such a good idea."

"Let's add prepackaged foods to the list," said Luis. "They are easy to preheat. They will be hot when the guests arrive."

"Nonsense!" snaps Tanya. "Home-cooked food is immeasurably better than the store-bought kind."

"Okay, you cook," replies Luis.

"Fine," says Tanya. "Now, should we order preprinted invitations? I think they might be too impersonal."

"It will be impossible to write them all by hand!" cries Luis. "We'd have to work nonstop for hours to make them!"

Circle and write the word that best completes each sentence.

1. Tanya and Luis have a _____prepared_____ shopping list.

   (prepared)   previewed   prepaid

2. Tanya is _____impatient_____ and wants to get going.

   impartial   impolite   (impatient)

3. Luis wants to add _____prepackaged_____ foods to the list.

   predated   preheated   (prepackaged)

4. "_____Nonsense_____," argues Tanya.

   nonstop   nonfiction   (nonsense)

5. "Should we send _____preprinted_____ invitations?" asks Tanya.

   presupposed   (preprinted)   prepackaged

6. Luis thinks it will be _____impossible_____ to write the invitations all by hand.

   immobile   (impossible)   immaterial

Harcourt

Who Was Poor Richard?

Write one sentence in each box below to answer the questions. Use the page number listed as a guide.

Page 222

What were almanacs, and why were they popular in colonial America?

Possible response: They were books containing tidbits of information, and they were popular because there wasn't much else to read.

Page 223

How was Benjamin Franklin's almanac different from the rest?

Possible response: It was humorous, it contained proverbs, and he wrote it under a pen name.

Page 227

What is Benjamin Franklin also famous for?

Possible response: He was a writer, inventor, and diplomat, and he helped write the Declaration of Independence.

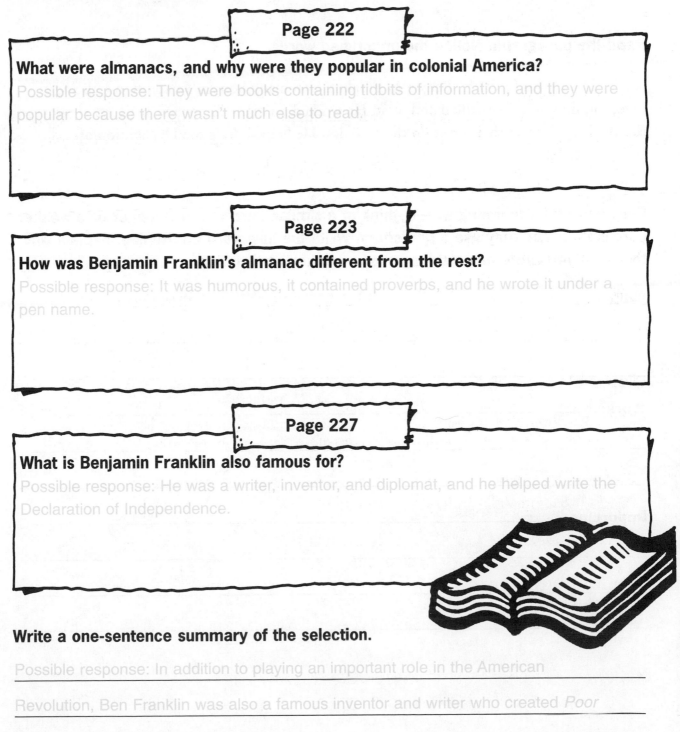

Write a one-sentence summary of the selection.

Possible response: In addition to playing an important role in the American

Revolution, Ben Franklin was also a famous inventor and writer who created *Poor*

Richard's Almanack.

Name _____

Connotation/Denotation

The dictionary definition of a word is its **denotation**. The feelings and ideas connected to a word and its meaning are called the **connotation**.

Read the paragraph. Notice the underlined words.

During his long life, Benjamin Franklin won many honors. In addition to being an inventor, he was a very <u>skilled</u> diplomat. He <u>worked</u> on many <u>important</u> matters. He got the British to repeal their taxes on the colonies. He helped <u>draft</u> the Declaration of Independence.

For each of the following words, think of a similar word with a stronger or a weaker connotation You may use a dictionary. Write the new word on the line. Explain why the word you wrote has a stronger or a weaker connotation.

Skilled _Possible response: capable; Capable has a weaker connotation than skilled._

Someone who is capable is more average than someone who is skilled.

_____

Worked _Possible response: labored; Labored has a stronger connotation than worked._

Someone who labored has probably done more than someone who simply worked.

_____

Important _Possible response: significant; Significant has a stronger connotation than_

important. I would pay attention to something that is significant before I would

pay attention to something that is important.

_____

Harcourt

Fluency Builder

profusely	many	expedition
ordeal	ago	station
terrain	along	mission
dismal	that	invention
peril	first	completion
esteem	faster	
	was	
	had	

1. Expeditions of explorers / reached California long ago.

2. The distance mail had to travel / was great / and the terrain / was rough.

3. Carrying the mail by stagecoach / was a dismal ordeal / that took weeks. / There were many perils / along the mail route.

4. The mission of the pony express / was simple— / to get news and mail to / California quickly.

5. The job held in highest esteem / was that of rider.

6. A rider on horseback / rode from station / to station.

7. The completion / of the first pony express mission / took 10 days.

8. Bands played, / and a cheering crowd thanked the rider profusely.

9. The invention of the telegraph / in 1837 / provided a faster way / to send news.

Harcourt

The Mission of the Pony Express

Circle the letter in front of the sentence that best describes the picture.

1 A Margaret uses caution when exploring.
  B Margaret has a passion for the sea.
  C Margaret visits the ranger station.

2 F She often takes vacations on her boat.
  G She studies bird migration.
  H She has a superstition about traveling.

3 A She planned an expedition down the coast.
  B She wrote letters on her best stationery.
  C She ignored the information.

4 F She followed the whale's migration.
  G She worked for the coastal institution.
  H She sailed to a far-off nation.

5 A She won the racing championship.
  B Her face showed her happy emotions.
  C Sometimes her boat was tossed by the waves.

6 F On occasion the waves were huge.
  G She felt elation when the storm passed.
  H She had to ration her supplies.

7 A In her opinion, sailing is boring.
  B Margaret made it back in good condition.
  C Margaret couldn't reach her destination.

Harcourt

Name_____

The Mission of the Pony Express

Write one sentence in each box below to show what you learned about the Pony Express.

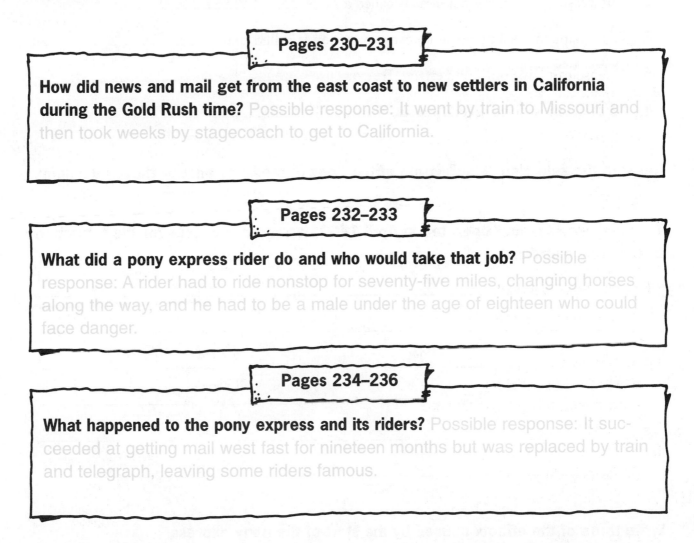

Pages 230–231

How did news and mail get from the east coast to new settlers in California during the Gold Rush time? Possible response: It went by train to Missouri and then took weeks by stagecoach to get to California.

Pages 232–233

What did a pony express rider do and who would take that job? Possible response: A rider had to ride nonstop for seventy-five miles, changing horses along the way, and he had to be a male under the age of eighteen who could face danger.

Pages 234–236

What happened to the pony express and its riders? Possible response: It succeeded at getting mail west fast for nineteen months but was replaced by train and telegraph, leaving some riders famous.

Now use the information in the boxes to write a one-sentence summary of the selection.

Possible response: In the mid-1800s, the pony express used brave boys and fast horses to get mail to the west coast quickly until trains and the telegraph took over.

Harcourt

Cause and Effect

Fill in the blanks.

1. The reason something happens is called a _____cause_____.

2. What happens as a result of an event or action is called the _____effect_____.

3. A cause can have only one effect. True or false? _____false_____

4. An effect must have several causes. True or false? _____false_____

Refer to the selection "The Mission of the Pony Express" to answer these questions.

The pony express first operated in April 1860. Write three causes for the formation of the pony express.

1. Many people moved west because of the Gold Rush.
   _____

2. Settlers in California wanted to get letters and news from home.
   _____

3. Stagecoach delivery was very slow.
   _____

Write three of the effects caused by the start of the pony express.

1. New jobs were created for people.
   _____

2. Brave boys got a chance to make good pay for their work.
   _____

3. Mail arrived on the west coast much faster.
   _____

Harcourt

Fluency Builder

designated	first	attended
installment	hill	children
exodus	across	trustingly
migrated	they	capable
burrowed	take	expected
family	helper	impossible
years	enough	

1. Two years ago / the family migrated / across the plains / in the great exodus / from the East.

2. The family's first home was burrowed / into the side of a hill.

3. Each child has designated chores / to do every day.

4. Children living on farms / are expected to be / capable helpers.

5. When the snow comes, / it will be impossible / to get to the schoolhouse.

6. The family earned / enough money to pay / the first installment / on the loan / they had taken / for the land.

7. At the schoolhouse / children are playing / Snap-the-Whip.

8. One teacher taught / children of all ages / who attended the one-room sod schoolhouse.

Frontier Children

Read the story. Then write the word from the story that best completes each sentence below it.

April and Danny are taking a photography class. April wants to learn how to take better pictures of wildflowers. Danny wants to learn how to develop his photos himself.

Last weekend April and Danny practiced taking pictures. They took a picnic basket to a meadow near their neighborhood. "I can't wait to start!" said April. "I see several flowers I want to photograph."

"I'm famished," said Danny. "I think I'll eat first and take photos later." He unpacked the picnic basket and began to munch on an apple.

Meanwhile, April walked around the meadow, snapping pictures nonstop. She did her best to remain motionless when she took each one, as her teacher had showed her. By the time Danny joined her, she had already gone through two rolls of film. "You're unbelievable!" Danny laughed when she showed him the rolls.

"Not really," April said. "I'm just determined to improve!"

1. April and Danny are taking a _____ photography _____ class.

2. They practiced taking photos last _____ weekend _____.

3. They went to a meadow near their _____ neighborhood _____.

4. When they got there, _____ April _____ started shooting pictures.

5. Danny was _____ famished _____, so he chose to eat first.

6. The first thing he ate was an _____ apple _____.

7. Meanwhile, April took pictures _____ nonstop _____.

8. Danny thought she was _____ unbelievable _____ for working so hard.

Now draw a line between the syllables of each word you wrote.

Harcourt

Frontier Children

Write one sentence in each box below to show what you learned about frontier life.

Pages 238–239

What is life like for frontier children? Possible response: The children rise early in the morning to do chores.

Pages 240–241

What challenges do newcomers to the frontier face? Possible response: They must adapt to the unfamiliar and desolate landscape, build a home out of sod, and start a farm.

Pages 242–243

What do the frontier children like about their new home? Possible response: They enjoy eating fresh food from the farm and making new friends at school.

Now use the information in the boxes to write a one-sentence summary of the selection.

Possible response: Although it was difficult to adjust to life on the frontier, families who settled there found ways to make it feel like home.

Summarize and Paraphrase

Fill in the blanks.

To summarize is to _____ tell the main points of a selection _____.

To paraphrase is to _____ retell the selection in your own words _____.

Read the following paragraph.

At first the children yawn and blink sleepily. Outside their sod home, however, their energy is restored by the fresh air, and they shiver in the early-morning chill. Fall comes early in this climate, and soon the grass will be covered with snow.

Write a summary of the above paragraph.

Possible responses: The children shiver when they walk out of their sod house and into the cold air. Fall is coming, and snow will soon cover the ground.

Read the following sentences.

The girl grabs a milk pail and a three-legged stool. Her designated chore is to milk the cow that waits in the small barn.

Write a paraphrase of the sentences above.

Possible responses: The girl picks up a stool and a milk pail. She has been asked to go to the barn and milk the cow.

Harcourt